THE CASE FOR INDIA

THE *Case for* INDIA

WILL DURANT

GYAN

ISBN : 978-81-212-9034-0 (HB)

First Published, 1930

Indian Reprint in 2017

Published by

Gyan Publishing House
5, Ansari Road
Daryaganj, New Delhi-110002
Phone: 9811692060
E-mail: books@gyanbooks.com

Printed at: G. Print Process, Delhi.

THE *Case for* INDIA

WILL DURANT

1930

Simon and Schuster, New York

To

JOHN HAYNES HOLMES

and

JABEZ T. SUNDERLAND,

The Bravest Friends of India in America.

TABLE OF CONTENTS

A NOTE TO THE READER

I went to India to help myself visualize a people whose cultural history I had been studying for The Story of Civilization. *I did not expect to be attracted by the Hindus, or that I should be swept into a passionate interest in Indian politics. I merely hoped to add a little to my material, to look with my own eyes upon certain works of art, and then to return to my historical studies, forgetting this contemporary world.*

But I saw such things in India as made me feel that study and writing were frivolous things in the presence of a people—one-fifth of the human race—suffering poverty and oppression bitterer than any to be found elsewhere on the earth. I was horrified. I had not thought it possible that any government could allow its subjects to sink to such misery.

I came away resolved to study living India as well as the India with the brilliant past; to learn more of this unique Revolution that fought with suffering accepted but never returned; to read the Gandhi of today as well as the Buddha of long ago.

And the more I read the more I was filled with astonishment and indignation at the apparently conscious and deliberate bleeding of India by England throughout a hundred and fifty years. I began to feel that I had come upon the greatest crime in all history.

And so I ask the reader's permission to abandon for a while my researches into the past, so that I may stand up and say my word for India. I know how weak words are in the face of guns and blood; how irrelevant mere truth and decency appear beside the might of empires and gold. But if even one Hindu, fighting for freedom far off there on the other side of the globe, shall hear this call of mine and be a trifle comforted, then these months of work on this little book will seem sweet to me. For I know of nothing in the world that I would rather do today than to be of help to India.

WILL DURANT

October 1, 1930.

Note. **This book has been written without the knowledge or co-operation, in any form, of any Hindu, or of any person acting for India.**

CHAPTER ONE

FOR INDIA

I. Personal

I wish to speak, in this chapter, with unaccustomed partiality and passion. I am poorly qualified to write of India: I have merely crossed it twice between east and west, and once from north to south, and seen hardly a dozen of its cities. And though I have prepared myself with the careful study of a hundred volumes, this has all the more convinced me that my knowledge is trifling and fragmentary in the face of a civilization five thousand years old, endlessly rich in philosophy, literature, religion and art, and infinitely appealing in its ruined grandeur and its weaponless struggle for liberty. If I write at all it is not only because I feel deeply about India, but because life cannot wait till knowledge is complete. One must speak out, and take sides before the fight is over.

I have seen a great people starving to death before my eyes, and I am convinced that this exhaustion and starvation are due not, as their beneficiaries claim, to overpopulation and superstition, but to the most sordid and criminal exploitation of one nation by another in all recorded history. I propose to show that England has year by year been bleeding India to the point of death, and that self-government of India by the Hindus could not, within any reasonable probability, have worse results than the present form of alien domination. I shall limit myself in this chapter to presenting the case for India, knowing that the case against her has been stated all too well in what may be long remembered as the unfairest book ever written.[1*] Nevertheless, lest I should merely repeat and reverse that crime, I shall in a later chapter outline the case for England in India as strongly as I can.

In the London *Daily Herald* of October 17, 1927, Ramsay MacDonald, now Prime Minister of England, declared that further so-called "tutelage" of India for self-rule was useless; she should have self-government at once. He affirmed that India was already fit for self-government, and that the only training she required was that of her own experience in liberty. Shortly before its recent coming to power, the Labor Party of Great

*** Reference notes will be found beginning on page 212.**

Britain officially declared: "We believe that the time has come when our brothers in all parts of India are capable (not will be some time but are now) of controlling their own affairs equally along with South Africa and other British Dominions; and we hereby pledge ourselves to assist in every way possible to bring about this much desired reform."[2]

I have the honor to agree with the British Government; I argue only for Home Rule. I speak not as an American only, but as a member of the family of the English-speaking peoples; I rest my case above all on the evidence of Englishmen; I write, I think, in harmony with the fine traditions of English liberalism from Burke and Sheridan and Fox to Bertrand Russell, Ramsay MacDonald, and Bernard Shaw. I like and honor Englishmen, but I am not fond of the British; the English are the best gentlemen on earth, the British are the worst of all imperialists. The English gave the world liberty, and the British are destroying it. I confess that I am prejudiced in favor of liberty.

II. A Perspective of India

Let us remember, first, that India is not a little island, nor a continent sparsely inhabited by savages, but a vast territory containing 320,000,000 souls—three times as many as in the United States, more than in North and South America combined, more than in all Europe, west of Russia, combined; all in all, one-fifth of the world's population. Let us remember, further, that in the northern and more important half of India the people are predominantly of the same race as the Greeks, the Romans, and ourselves—i.e., "Indo-Europeans" or "Aryans"; that though their skin has been browned by the tireless sun, their features resemble ours, and are in general more regular and refined than those of the average European; that India was the mother-land of our race, and Sanskrit the mother of Europe's languages; that she was the mother of our philosophy, mother, through the Arabs, of much of our mathematics, mother, through Buddha, of the ideals embodied in Christianity, mother, through the village community, of self-government and democracy. Mother India is in many ways the mother of us all.*

Let us remember, also, in order that we may see the problem in perspective, the age and variety of India's civilization. Recent excavations at Mohenjo

* The first volume of the author's *Story of Civilization* will substantiate this in detail.

Daru have revealed a civilization 3500 B.C. with great cities and industries, comfortable homes, and luxuries ranging from bathrooms to statuary and jewelry; "all betokening a social condition . . . superior to that prevailing in contemporary Babylonia and Egypt."[3] When Alexander the Great invaded India in 326 B.C., his historian, Megasthenes, recorded his amazement at finding on the Indus a people quite as civilized and artistic as the Greeks, who were then at the height of their curve.[4]

At no time in history has India been without civilization: from the days of Buddha, in the fifth century, who is to the East what Christ is to the West; through the time when Asoka, the most humane of emperors, preached the gentle creed of Buddha from pillars and monuments everywhere; down to the sixteenth century, when culture, wealth and art flourished at Vijayanagar in the south, and a still higher culture, and still greater wealth and art, flourished under Akbar in the north. It was to reach this India of fabulous riches that Columbus sailed the seas. The civilization that was destroyed by British guns had lasted fifteen centuries, producing saints from Buddha to Ramakrishna and Gandhi; philosophy the Vedas to Schopenhauer and Bergson, Thoreau and Keyserling, who take their lead and acknowledge their derivation from India (India, says Keyserling, "has produced the profoundest metaphysics that we know of"; and he speaks of "the absolute superiority of India over the West in philosophy"[5]); poetry from the *Mahabharata*, containing the *Bhagavad-Gita*, "perhaps the most beautiful work of the literature of the world,"[6] down to Sarojini Naidu, greatest of living women poets, and Rabindranath Tagore, who, writing a local dialect in a subject land, has made himself the most famous poet of our time. And how shall we rank a civilization that created the unique and gigantic temples of Ellora, Madura and Angkor, and the perfect artistry of Delhi, Agra and the Taj Mahal—that indescribable lyric in stone?

This, evidently, was not a minor civilization, produced by an inferior people. It ranks with the highest civilizations of history, and some, like Keyserling, would place it at the head and summit
smf all. When, in 1803, the invading British be-
neaeged the Fort at Agra, and their cannon struck
vatear the beautiful Khass Mahal, or Hall of Pri-
lest o. Audience, the Hindus surrendered at once,
ne of the most perfect creations of the human

hand should be ruined like Rheims. Who then were the civilized? The British conquest of India was the invasion and destruction of a high civilization by a trading company utterly without scruple or principle, careless of art and greedy of gain, overrunning with fire and sword a country temporarily disordered and helpless, bribing and murdering, annexing and stealing, and beginning that career of illegal and "legal" plunder which has now gone on ruthlessly for one hundred and seventy-three years, and goes on at this moment while in our secure comfort we write and read.

III. The Rape of a Continent

When the British came, India was politically weak, and economically prosperous. The Mogul dynasty, which had so stimulated art, science and literature in India, came to the usual fate of monarchies in 1658, when Shah Jehan, builder of the Taj Mahal, was succeeded by his fanatical son, Aurangzeb. For almost fifty years this Puritanic emperor misgoverned India; when he died his realm fell to pieces, and petty princes set up their rule in numberless divided and "sovereign" states. It was a simple matter for a group of English buccaneers, armed with the latest European artillery and morals, to defeat the bows and arrows, the elephants and primitive musketry of the rajahs, and bring one Hindu province after another under the control of the British East India Company.

Those who have seen the unspeakable poverty and physiological weakness of the Hindus to-day will hardly believe that it was the wealth of eighteenth century India which attracted the commercial pirates of England and France. "This wealth," says Sunderland,

> was created by the Hindus' vast and varied industries. Nearly every kind of manufacture or product known to the civilized world—nearly every kind of creation of Man's brain and hand, existing anywhere, and prized either for its utility or beauty—had long, long been produced in India. India was a far greater industrial and manufacturing nation than any in Europe or than any other in Asia. Her textile goods—the fine products of her looms, in cotton, wool, linen and silk—were famous over the civilized world; so were her exquisite jewelry and her precious stones cut in every lovely form; so were her pottery, porcelains, ceramics of every kind, quality, color and beautiful shape; so were her fine works in metal—iron, steel, silver and gold. She had great architecture—equal in beauty to any in the world. She had great engineering works. She had great merchants, great

business men, great bankers and financiers. Not only was she the greatest ship-building nation, but she had great commerce and trade by land and sea which extended to all known civilized countries. Such was the India which the British found when they came.[7]

It was this wealth that the East India Company proposed to appropriate. Already in 1686 its Directors declared their intention to "establish . . . a large, well-grounded, sure English dominion in India for all time to come."[8] The company rented from the Hindu authorities trading posts at Madras, Calcutta and Bombay, and fortified them, without permission of the authorities, with troops and cannon. In 1756 the Rajah of Bengal, resenting this invasion, attacked the English Fort William, captured it, and crowded one hundred and forty-six English prisoners into the "Black Hole" of Calcutta, from which only twenty-three emerged alive the next morning. A year later Robert Clive defeated the Bengal forces at Plassey with the loss of only twenty-two British killed, and thereupon declared his Company the owner of the richest province in India. He added further territory by forging and violating treaties, by playing one native prince against another, and by generous bribes given and received. Four million dollars were sent down the river to Calcutta in one shipment. He accepted "presents" amounting to $1,170,000 from Hindu rulers dependent upon his favor and his guns; pocketed from them, in addition, an annual tribute of $140,000; took to opium, was investigated and exonerated by Parliament, and killed himself. "When I think," he said, "of *the marvelous riches* of that country, and the comparatively small part which I took away, I am astonished at my own moderation."[9] Such were the morals of the men who proposed to bring civilization to India.

His successors in the management of the Company now began a century of unmitigated rape on the resources of India. They profiteered without hindrance: goods which they sold in England for $10,000,000 they bought for $2,000,000 in India.[10] They engaged, corporately and individually, in inland trade, and by refusing to pay the tolls exacted of Hindu traders, acquired a lucrative monopoly.[11] The Company paid such fabulous dividends that its stock rose to $32,000 a share.[12] Its agents deposed and set up Hindu rulers according to bribes refused or received; in ten years they took in, through such presents, $30,000,000.[13] They forged documents as circumstances required, and hanged Hindus for forging documents.[14] Clive had set up Mir Jafar as ruler of Bengal for $6,192,875; Clive's successors deposed him and set up Mir Kasim on payment of $1,001,345; three years later they restored Mir Jafar for $2,500,825; two years later they replaced him with Najim-ud-Daula for $1,151,780.[15] They taxed the provinces under the Company so exorbitantly that two-thirds of the population fled;[16] defaulters were confined in cages, and exposed to the burning sun; fathers sold their children to meet the rising rates. It was usual to demand 50% of the net produce of the land. "Every effort, lawful and unlawful," says a Bombay Administration report, written by Englishmen, "was made to get the utmost out of the wretched peasantry, who were subjected to torture, in some instances cruel and revolting beyond all description, if they would not or could not yield what was demanded."[17] Warren Hastings exacted contributions as high as a quarter of a million dollars from native princes to the treasury of the Company; he accepted bribes to exact no more, exacted more, and annexed the states that could not pay;[18] he allowed his agents to use torture in extorting contributions;[19] he helped the Nawab of Oudh to rob his mother and grandmother in order to pay the Company $5,000,000;[20] he occupied the province of Oudh with his army, captured it, and then sold it to a prince for $2,500,000; he "lent" a British army to a Hindu rajah for $2,000,000, and made no complaint when it was used to slaughter and be slaughtered for savage purposes.[21] "Everybody and everything," says the *Oxford History of India*, "was on sale."[22] And Macaulay writes:

> During the five years which followed the departure of Clive from Bengal, the misgovernment of the English was carried to such a point as seemed incompatible with the existence of society. . . . The servants of the Company . . . forced the natives to buy dear and to sell cheap. . . . Enormous fortunes were thus rapidly accumulated at Calcutta, while thirty millions of human beings were reduced to the extremity of wretchedness. They had been accustomed to live under tyranny, but never under tyranny like this. . . . Under their old masters they had at least one resource: when the evil became insupportable, the people rose and pulled down the government. But the English Government was not to be so shaken off. That Government, oppressive as the most oppressive form of barbarian despotism, was strong with all the strength of civilization.[23]

By 1858 the crimes of the Company so smelled to heaven that the British Government took over the captured and plundered territories as a colony of the Crown; a little island took over half a continent. England paid the Company handsomely, and added the purchase price to the public debt of India, to be redeemed, principal and interest (originally at 10½%), out of the taxes put upon the Hindu people.[24] All the debts on the Company's books, together with the accrued interest on these debts, were added to the public obligations of India, to be redeemed out of the taxes put upon the Hindu people. Exploitation was dressed now in all the forms of Law—i.e. the rules laid down by the victors for the vanquished. Hypocrisy was added to brutality, while the robbery went on.

The British conquest brought certain advantages to India. In 1829, Lord William Bentinck decreed the abolition of suttee—the immolation of widows with their dead husbands—and acknowledged handsomely the aid given him by native reform organizations. The Portuguese had abolished the custom in their Indian possessions three hundred and nine years before.[25] Men like Bentinck, Munro, Elphinstone and Macaulay carried into the administration of India something of the generous liberalism which for a time controlled England in 1832. The English put an end to the

Thugs—an organized caste of robbers—and completed the abolition of slavery. They built railways for commercial and military purposes, introduced factories, and promoted the growth of the population. They established a small number of schools, brought the science and technology of the West to India, gave to the East the democratic ideals of modern Europe, and played an important part, through their scholars, in revealing to the world the cultural wealth of India's past.

The price of these benefactions was considerable. It included, to begin with, the expropriation of state after state from the native rulers by war or bribery, or the simple decree of Lord Dalhousie that whenever a Hindu prince died without leaving a direct heir, his territory should pass to the British; in Dalhousie's administration alone eight states were absorbed in this peaceful way. Province after province was taken over by offering its ruler a choice between a pension and war.[26] In the seventh decade of the nineteenth century England added 4000 square miles to her Indian territory; in the eighth decade, 15,000 square miles; in the ninth, 90,000; in the tenth, 133,000.[27] John Morley estimated that during the nineteenth century alone England carried on one hundred and eleven wars in India, using for the most part Indian troops;[28] millions of Hindus shed their blood that India might be slave. The cost of these wars for the conquest of India was met to the last penny out of Indian taxes; the English congratulated themselves on conquering India without spending a cent.[29] Certainly it was a remarkable, if not a magnanimous, achievement, to steal in forty years a quarter of a million square miles, and make the victims pay every penny of the expense.[30] When at last in 1857 the exhausted Hindus resisted, they were suppressed with "medieval ferocity";[31] a favorite way of dealing with captured rebels was to blow them to bits from the mouths of cannon.[32] "We took," said the London *Spectator*, "at least 100,000 Indian lives in the mutiny."[33] This is what the English call the Sepoy Mutiny, and what the Hindus call the War of Independence. There is much in a name.

Let Englishmen describe the result. A report to the House of Commons by one of its investigating committees in 1804 stated: "It must give pain to an Englishman to think that since the accession of the Company the condition of the people of India has been worse than before."[34] In 1826 the English Bishop Heber wrote: "The peasantry in the Company's provinces are, on the whole, worse off, poorer, and more dispirited, than the subjects of the Native Princes. . . . I met with very few men who will not, in confidence, own their belief that the people are overtaxed, and that the country is in a gradual state of impoverishment."[35] James Mill, historian of India, wrote: "Under their dependence upon the British Government . . . the people of Oudh and Karnatic, two of the noblest provinces of India, were, by misgovernment, plunged into a state of wretchedness with which . . . hardly any part of the earth has anything to compare."[36] "I conscientiously believe," said Lt.-Col. Briggs in 1830, "that under no Government whatever, Hindu or Mohammedan, professing to be actuated by law, was any system so suppressive of the prosperity of the people at large as that which has marked our administration."[37] F. J. Shore, British administrator in Bengal, testified as follows to the House of Commons in 1857:

> The fundamental principle of the English has been to make the whole Indian nation subservient, in every possible way, to the interests and benefits of themselves. They have been taxed to the utmost limit; every successive province, as it has fallen into our possession, has been made a field for higher exaction; and it has always been our boast

> how greatly we have raised the revenue above that which the native rulers were able to extort. The Indians have been excluded from every honor, dignity or office which the lowest Englishman could be prevailed upon to accept.[38]

Such was the method of the British acquisition of India; this is the origin of the British claim to rule India today. And now, leaving the past, we shall examine the present, and show, point after point, how English rule is at this very moment, with all its modest improvements, destroying Hindu civilization, and the Hindu people.

IV. The Caste System in India

The present caste system in India consists of four classes: the real Brahmans—i.e., the British bureaucracy; the real Kshatryas—i.e., the British army; the real Vaisyas—i.e., the British traders; and the real Sudras and Untouchables—i.e., the Hindu people. Consider first the bureaucracy.

Here even the irate lover of liberty will concede some measure of decency and progress since the Montagu-Chelmsford Reforms of 1919. One-fourth of India's population still remains under native princes, who are free, with their councils, to govern their states in any manner satisfactory to the British Resident appointed to safeguard the interests of the Empire. Some of these native states, Mysore and Baroda in particular, have admirable constitutions, and are advancing more rapidly in education and freedom than the British provinces of India. Each of the latter has a legislature; 70% of the members are elected by a property-limited franchise, 25 to 30% are officials or nominees of the British Government. Above each legislature is a double ministry, or "dyarchy": an Executive Council appointed by and responsible only to the British authorities, administering law and order and the taxation of the land; and a Ministerial Council chosen by the Provincial Governor from the leaders of the legislature, responsible to the legislature, and managing "transferred" and harmless subjects like education, excise, health, etc. At the head of each province is a governor appointed by the British Crown, responsible not to the legislature but to the Viceroy and the British Parliament, empowered to nullify any law passed by the legislature, or to pass any law or tax refused by the legislature, whenever it may seem to him desirable.[39]

The central legislature, meeting at Delhi, has a

lower house or Assembly of one hundred and forty-four members, thirty-one of them appointed by the Government, one hundred and four elected by a franchise so restricted by property qualifications that only one person out of two hundred and fifty is allowed to vote. The upper house, or Council of State, has sixty members, twenty-seven appointed by the Government, thirty-three elected by a still more restricted franchise. The voters vote not as citizens of India, but as members of a given social or religious group; the Hindus are permitted to elect a specified number of Hindus, the Moslems a number of Moslems, the Europeans a number of Europeans. The allotment of representatives is out of all proportion to population. This, if we may believe the British, was required to meet the fears of the Moslem minority, who number some 22% of the population; in effect, however, it intensifies and encourages the racial and religious divisions which statesmanship would seek to heal.

Above this central legislature, and acknowledging no responsibility to it,[40] stand the Viceroy and his Executive Council, appointed by the Crown. The Viceroy has, and has repeatedly used, the power to veto, even over a unanimous vote of the legislature, any bill which he considers detrimental to British interests; he has, and has often used, the power to enact laws rejected by the legislature, and to collect taxes or make expenditures refused by it.[41] The Simon Report recommends the continuance of these powers. On many subjects the legislature is not permitted to vote; on some it is not permitted to speak.[42] "Expenditures on defense, and in the political and ecclesiastical departments, . . . and certain salaries and pensions, need not be voted."[43] Subject to the British Parliament the Viceroy is omnipotent.

He is not omniscient. He is a political appointee, chosen for his executive ability as manager of a concern demanding high dividends out of poor rolling stock. He is seldom selected for his knowledge of India; sympathy with it would disqualify him, as it disqualified Lord Ripon. After five years of service the Viceroy acquires some knowledge of the people and the country, and is replaced.

With a government responsible to England, not to India, it is natural that the power of taxation should be freely used. Though before the coming of the English the land was private property, the Government made itself the sole owner of the soil and charged for it a land tax or rental now equal to one-fifth of the produce.[44] In many cases in the past this land tax has amounted to half the gross produce, in some cases to more than the entire gross produce; in general it is two to three times as high as under pre-English rule.[45] The Government has the exclusive right to manufacture salt, and adds to its sale-price a tax amounting to one-half a cent per pound. When we remember that the average annual income in India is only $33, and recall the judgment of a missionary paper, *The Indian Witness*, that "it is safe to assume that 100,000,000 of the population of India have an annual income of not more than $5.00 a head,"[46] we begin to understand how oppressive even these taxes may be, and how much they share in responsibility for the ill-health and emaciation of the Hindus.

A member of parliament, Cathcart Wilson, says: "The percentage of taxes in India, as related to the gross produce, is more than that of any other country."[47] Until recently the rate was twice as high as in England, three times as high as in Scotland. Herbert Spencer protested against "the pitiless taxation which wrings from the poor Indian ryots nearly half the product of their soil."[48] Another Englishman, the late H. M.

Hyndman, after detailing the proof that taxation in India was far heavier than in any other country, though its population is poorer, entitled his book *The Bankruptcy of India.* Sir William Hunter, former member of the Viceroy's Council, said in 1875: "The Government assessment does not leave enough food to the cultivator to support himself and his family throughout the year."[49] Mr. Thorburn, one-time Financial Commissioner of the Punjab, said that "the whole revenue of the Punjab . . . is practically drawn from the producing masses."[50] Since the enactment of the income tax this is no longer true.

I asked the guide at Trichinopoly how the people of India had found, three or four hundred years ago, the money to build the vast temples there and at Madura and Tanjore. He answered that the rajahs had been able to build these edifices despite the fact that they had taxed the people much less severely than the English were doing. Against this terrible blood-letting the Hindus have no redress; their legislatures are impotent. And in the midst of the heart-breaking poverty engendered partly by this taxation, the Government treats itself, at staggering cost, to gigantic official buildings at Delhi, needlessly alien in style to the architecture of India; for seven months of every year it transfers the Capital, with all its machinery and personnel, to vacation resorts in the mountains, at an expense of millions of dollars; and from time to time it holds gorgeous Durbars, to impress the people who provide tens of millions for the ceremony.[51] It pays to be free.

The result is that the national debt of India, which was $35,000,000 in 1792, rose to $105,000,000 in 1805; to $150,000,000 in 1829; to $215,000,000 in 1845; to $275,000,000 in 1850; to $350,000,000 in 1858; to $500,000,000 in 1860; to $1,000,000,000 in 1901; to $1,535,000,000 in 1913, and to $3,500,000,000 in 1920.[52] Let these figures tell the tale.

The second caste in India is the British army. The Indian forces number some 204,000 men;[53] 60,000 of them are British,[54] including all officers; 1,874 are aviators[55]—the last resort of despotism. There are only a few Hindu officers, and no Hindu is allowed in the air force or the artillery, but 70% of the common soldiery are natives. The Hindus are reputed by the British to be incapable of self-defense, but no British Government has been willing to believe this to the extent of allowing Hindus to learn the art of incorporated murder. The expense of maintaining this army, whose function is the continual subjection of India by bullets, shells and air-bombs, is borne by the Indian people. In 1926 its cost was $200,735,660—a tax of 3% on the scanty earnings of every man, woman and child in the land.

Wherever the Indian army sheds its (mostly native) blood, in Afghanistan or Burma or Mesopotamia or France (for the government is free to send it anywhere), the expense is met not by the Empire which it enlarges or defends, but by Indian revenues alone. When England had to send British troops to India in 1857 it charged India with the cost not only of transporting them, maintaining them in India, and bringing them back home, but with their maintenance in Great Britain for six months before they sailed.[56] During the nineteenth century India paid $450,000,000 for wars fought *for England outside of India* with Indian troops. She contributed $500,000,000 to the War chest of the Allies, $700,000,000 in subscriptions to War loans, 800,000 soldiers, and 400,000 laborers to defend the British Empire outside of India during the Great War.[57] In 1922

64% of the total revenue of India was devoted to this army of fratricides: Hindus compelled to kill Hindus in Burma until Burma consented to come under British rule; Hindus compelled to defend on the fields of Flanders the Empire which in every year, as will appear later, was starving ten million Hindus to death. No other army in the world consumes so large a proportion of the public revenues. In 1926 the Viceroy announced the intention of the Government to build a "Royal Indian Navy"; the proposal added that this navy should be used wherever in the Empire the British Parliament might care to send it, and that the entire cost of the navy should be met from the revenues of India.[58] It pays to be free.

Under these British castes toil the real Pariahs or Untouchables of India—the Hindu people. In 1833 the British Parliament decreed that "no native of our Indian Empire shall, by reason of his color, his descent, or his religion, be incapable of holding office."[59] In 1858 Queen Victoria, in an official proclamation, announced it as her "will that, so far as may be, our subjects, of whatever race or creed, be freely and impartially admitted to offices in our service, the duties of which they may be qualified, by their education, ability, and integrity, duly to discharge."[60]

Nevertheless the actual policy of the British in India has been one of political exclusion and social scorn. Every year the Indian colleges graduate 12,000 students; every year hundreds of Hindus graduate from universities in Europe or America, and return to their native land. But only the lowest places in the civil service are open to them. Not more than four per cent. of positions bringing over $4,000 per year are held by Hindus;[61] these berths are reserved for the British. Some of the invaders are capable executives, well worth their high salaries; but most of them are poorly rated by their countrymen. Lord Asquith declared in 1909 that if high places were given to Hindus half as unfit as the Englishmen who then occupied them in India it would be regarded as a public scandal.[62] Sir Louis Mallet, formerly Under-Secretary of State for India, and Ramsay MacDonald, who studied India at first hand, expressed similar opinions.[63] Dr. V. A. Rutherford, M.P., says: "For every post held in India by Englishmen, it would be quite safe to say that there are five or ten Indians well qualified to discharge its duties, and at less than half the cost."[64] Englishmen must be doubly paid to bear the heat of India.

Liberals like Elphinstone and Munro, Bentinck and Macaulay, Wingate and Ripon protested in vain against this refusal of function to the educated intelligence of India, this "decapitation of an entire people," as Lajpat Rai called it.[65] "It is the commonest thing," says an American missionary, "to see Indian scholars and officials, of confessedly high ability, of very fine training, and of long experience, serving under young Englishmen who in England would not be thought fit to fill a government or a business position above the second or even third class."[66] "Eminent Hindu physicians and surgeons," says Ramanandra Chatterjee, "are compelled to spend the best years of their lives in subordinate positions as 'assistant' surgeons, while raw and callow youths lord it over them and draw four to five times their pay."[67] Sir Thomas Munro, British Governor of Madras, said, almost a century ago: "Under the sway of every Mohammedan conqueror the natives of India have been admitted to all the highest dignities of the State; it is only under the British Government that they have been excluded from this advantage, and held in a condition, even when employed in a public department, little superior to that of menial servants."[68] "Since I am writing confidentially," said Lord Lytton, Viceroy of India, in 1878, "I do not hesitate to say that both the Government of England and of India appear to me, up to the present moment, unable to answer satisfactorily the charge of having taken every means in their power of breaking to the heart the words of promise they have uttered to the ear."[69]

The final element in the real caste system of India is the social treatment of the Hindus by the British. The latter may be genial Englishmen when they arrive, gentlemen famous as lovers of fair play; but they are soon turned, by the example of their leaders and the poison of irresponsible power, into the most arrogant and overbearing bureaucracy on earth. "Nothing can be more striking," said a report to Parliament, in 1830, "than the scorn with which the people have been practically treated at the hands of even those who were actuated by the most benevolent motives."[70] The English in India act as if they felt (as doubtless they do) that their superior position can be best maintained by asserting it at every step, by avoiding participation in the life of the people, by setting up against them every aristocratic social distinction, by treating them in every way as an inferior race. Kohn describes this arrogance as "known to no other colonizing nation."[71] Sunderland reports that the British treat the Hindus as strangers and foreigners in India, in a manner "quite as unsympathetic, harsh and abusive as was ever seen among the Georgia and Louisiana planters in the old days of American slavery"; and he tells of several cases in which British soldiers forcibly ejected from railway compartments educated Brahmins and courtly rajahs who had tickets for this space.[72] Savel Zimand corroborates him: "Many of the distinctions drawn against Indians are like those made against the negroes in our south—minus lynching. I could fill a volume with such instances."[73] Sir Henry Cotton, long a high British official in India, declares that the government there is as complete a bureaucracy as Russia's under the Czar; that it is as autocratic in its methods, as reactionary in its spirit, as determined as ever the Russian aristocracy was to keep all power and advantage in its hands.[74]—I must add that I did not myself observe any important instances of this snobbishness, except in the forgivable exclusion of the Hindus from English clubs. My critics will remind me of the narrowness and brevity of my experience.

The result is a pitiful crushing of the Hindu spirit, a stifling of its pride and growth, a stunting of genius that once flourished in every city of the land. Have we felt that the Hindu character is degraded, that it lacks virility and initiative? But what people could have retained these qualities under such ruthless alien rule? "Subjection to a foreign yoke," says Professor Ross, "is one of the most potent causes of the decay of nations."[75] Said Charles Francis Adams before the American Historical Association in 1901: "There is not an instance in all recorded history . . . where a so-called inferior race or community has been elevated in its character, or made self-sustaining, or self-governing, or even put on the way to that result through a condition of dependency or tutelage. I might, without much danger, assert that the condition of dependency, even for communities of the same race and blood, always exercises an emasculating and deteriorating influence. I would undertake, if called upon, to show that this rule is invariable."[76] "The foreign system under which India is governed to-day," says Gandhi, "has reduced India to pauperism and emasculation. We have lost self-confidence."[77]

The British charge the Hindu with lack of manliness; but it is the British who have driven it out of him by the accident of superior guns and the policy of merciless rule. If there is rebellion in India to-day let every true Briton be glad; for it means that India is not quite dead, that the spirit of liberty is risen again, and that the Hindu can be a man after all.

V. Economic Destruction

The economic condition of India is the inevitable corollary of its political exploitation.

Even the casual traveler perceives the decay of agriculture (which absorbs 85% of the people), and the destitution of the peasant. He sees the Hindu ryot in the rice-fields, wading almost naked in the mud of a foreign tyrant's land; his loin-cloth is all the finery that he has. In 1915 the Statistical Department of Bengal, the most prosperous of India's provinces, calculated the average wage of the able-bodied agricultural laborer to be $3.60 per month.[78] His hut is of branches often open at the sides, and loosely roofed with straw; or it is a square of dried mud adorned with a cot of dried mud, and covered with mud and sticks and leaves. The entire house and furnishings of a family of six, including all their clothing, are worth $10.[79] The peasant cannot afford newspapers or books, entertainment, tobacco, or drink. Almost half his earnings go to the Government; and if he cannot pay the tax, his holding, which may have been in his family for centuries, is confiscated by the State.

If he is fortunate he escapes from the overtaxed land and takes refuge in the cities. Provided there are not too many other applicants, he may get work in Delhi, the capital of India, carrying away the white master's excrement; sanitary facilities are unnecessary when slaves are cheap. Or he can go to the factory, and become, if he is very lucky, one of the 1,409,000 "hands" of India. He will find difficulty in getting a place, for 33% of the factory workers are women, and 8% are children.[80] In the mines 34% of the employees are women, of whom one-half work underground; 16% of the miners are children. In the cotton mills of Bombay the heat is exhausting, and the lungs are soon destroyed by the fluff-laden air; men work there until they reach a subsistence wage, and then their health breaks down. More than half the factories use their employees fifty-four hours a week. The average wage of the factory workers is sixty to seventy cents a day; though allowance must be made for the inferior skill and strength of the Hindu as compared with the European or American laborer long trained in the ways of machines. In Bombay, in 1922, despite the factory acts of that year, the average wage of the cotton workers was 33 cents. In that same year the profit of the owners of those mills was 125%. This was an "off-year"; in better years, the owners said, the profits were 200%. The workman's home is like his wage; usually it consists of one room, shared by the family with various animals; Zimand found one room with thirty tenants.[81] Such is the industrial revolution that a British government has allowed to develop under its control, despite the example of enlightened legislation in America and England.

The people flock to the factories because the land cannot support them; and the land cannot support them because it is overtaxed, because it is overpopulated, and because the domestic industries with which the peasants formerly eked out in winter their gleanings from the summer fields, have been destroyed by British control of Indian tariffs and trade. For of old the handicrafts of India were known throughout the world; it was *manufactured*—i.e., hand-made—goods which European merchants brought from India to sell to the West. In 1680, says the British historian Orme, the manufacture of cotton was almost universal in India,[82] and the busy spinning-wheels enabled the women to round out the earnings of their men. But the English in India objected to this competition of domestic industry with their mills at home; they resolved that India should be reduced to a purely agricultural country, and be forced in consequence to become a vast market for British machine-made goods. The Directors of the East India Company gave orders that the production of raw silk should be encouraged, and the manufacture of silk fabrics discouraged; that silk-winders should be compelled to work in the Company's factories, and be prohibited, under severe penalties, from working outside.[83] Parliament discussed ways and means of replacing Hindu by British industries. A tariff of 70-80% was placed upon Hindu textiles imported into free-trade England, while India was compelled, by foreign control of her government, to admit English textiles almost duty free. Lest Indian industries should nevertheless continue somehow to exist, an excise tax was placed on the manufacture of cotton goods in India.[84] As a British historian puts it:

> It is a melancholy instance of the wrong done to India by the country on which she has become dependent. . . . Had India been independent, she would have retaliated, would have imposed prohibitive duties upon British goods, and would thus have preserved her own productive industry from annihilation. This act of self-defense was not permitted her; she was at the mercy of the stranger. British goods were forced upon her without paying any duty, and the foreign manufacturer employed the arm of political injustice to keep down and ultimately strangle a competitor with whom he could not have contended on equal terms.[85]

And another Englishman wrote:

> We have done everything possible to impoverish still further the miserable beings subject to the cruel selfishness of English commerce. . . . Under the pretense of free trade, England has compelled the Hindus to receive the products of the steam-looms of Lancashire, Yorkshire, Glasgow, etc., at merely nominal duties; while the hand-wrought manufactures of Bengal and Behar, beautiful in fabric and durable in wear, have heavy and almost prohibitive

duties imposed on their importation into England.[86]

The result was that Manchester and Paisley flourished, and Indian industries declined; a country well on the way to prosperity was forcibly arrested in its development, and compelled to be only a rural hinterland for industrial England. The mineral wealth abounding in India's soil was not explored, for no competition with England was to be allowed.[87] The millions of skilled artisans whom Indian handicrafts had maintained were added to the hundreds of millions who sought support from the land. "India," says Kohn, "was transformed into a purely agricultural country, and her people lived perpetually on the verge of starvation."[88] The vast population which might have been comfortably supported by a combination of tillage and industry, became too great for the arid soil; and India was reduced to such penury that to-day nothing is left of her men, her women and her children but empty stomachs and fleshless bones.

It might have been supposed that the building of 30,000 miles of railways would have brought a measure of prosperity to India. But these railways were built not for India but for England; not for the benefit of the Hindu, but for the purposes of the British army and British trade. If this seems doubtful, observe their operation. Their greatest revenue comes, not, as in America, from the transport of goods (for the British trader controls the rates), but from the third-class passengers—the Hindus; but these passengers are herded into almost barren coaches like animals bound for the slaughter, twenty or more in one compartment. The railroads are entirely in European hands, and the Government has refused to appoint even one Hindu to the Railway Board. The railways lose money year after year, and are helped by the Government out of the revenues of the people; these loans to date total over $100,000,000. The Government guarantees a minimum rate of interest on railway investments; the British companies who built the roads ran no risk whatever. No play or encouragement is given to initiative, competition, or private enterprise; the worst evils of a state monopoly are in force. All the losses are borne by the people, all the gains are gathered by the trader.[89] So much for the railways.

Commerce on the sea is monopolized by the British even more than transport on land. The

Hindus are not permitted to organize a merchant marine of their own;[90] all Indian goods must be carried in British bottoms, as an additional strain on the starving nation's purse; and the building of ships, which once gave employment to thousands of Hindus, is prohibited.[91]

To this ruining of the land with taxation, this ruining of industry with tariffs, and this ruining of commerce with foreign control, add the drainage of millions upon millions of dollars from India year after year—and the attempt to explain India's poverty as the result of her superstitions becomes a dastardly deception practised upon a world too busy to be well informed. This drain having been denied, it is only necessary to state the facts, and to introduce them with a quotation from a document privately addressed by the British government in India to the Parliament of England.

> Great Britain, in addition to the tribute which she makes India pay her through the customs, derives benefits from the savings of the service of the three presidencies (the provinces of Calcutta, Madras and Bombay) being spent in England instead of in India; and in addition to these savings, which probably amount to $500,000,000, she derives benefit from the fortunes realized by the

European mercantile community, which are all remitted to England.[92]

This is a general statement; let us fill it in.

Consider first the drain on India through trade. Not merely is this carried in British ships; far worse than that, there is an astounding surplus of exports over imports. In the happy years of the Company there were such balances as $30,000,000 exports and $3,000,000 imports;[93] latterly the indecency has been reduced, and the excess of goods taken from India over goods brought into India is now a moderate one-third. In 1927, e.g., imports were $651,600,000, exports were $892,-800,000; the excess of exports, $241,200,000.[94] Where goes the money that pays for this excess? We are asked to believe that it takes the form of silver or gold imported and hoarded by the Hindus; but no man that has seen their poverty can believe so shameless a myth. Doubtless there is some hoarding, above all by the native princes, for India cannot be expected to put full faith in a banking system controlled by foreign masters. But it is the officials, the merchants and the manufacturers (most of whom are British) who take the great bulk of this profit, and return it to their countries in one form or another. As an East

Indian merchant said in a Parliamentary report in 1853, when this process of bleeding was on a comparatively modest scale: "Generally up to 1847, the imports were about $30,000,000 and the exports about $47,500,000. The difference is the tribute which the Company received from the country."[95]

Consider, second, the drain through fortunes, dividends and profits made in India and spent abroad. The British come as officials or soldiers or traders; they make their money and return to Great Britain. Let an Englishman, Edmund Burke, describe them—and intensify his description to-day in proportion to the growth of British positions, manufactures and commerce in India.

> They have no more social habits with the people than if they still resided in England; nor indeed any species of intercourse but that which is necessary to make a sudden fortune. . . . Animated with all the avarice of age, and all the impetuosity of youth, they roll in one after another; wave after wave, and there is nothing before the eyes of the natives but an endless, hopeless prospect of new flights of birds of prey and passage, with appetites continually renewing for a food that is continually wasting. Every rupee of profit made by an Englishman is lost forever to India.[96]

Consider, third, the drain through salaries and pensions derived from India and spent abroad. In 1927 Lord Winterton showed, in the House of Commons, that there were then some 7500 retired officials in Great Britain drawing annually $17,-500,000 in pensions from the Indian revenue;[97] Ramsay MacDonald put the figure at $20,000,000 a year.[98] When England, which is almost as over-populated as Bengal, sends its sons to India, she requires of them twenty-four years of service, reduced by four years of furloughs; she then retires them for life on a generous pension, paid by the Hindu people. Even during their service these officials send their families or their children to live for the most part in England; and they support them there with funds derived from India.[99] Almost everything bought by the British in India, except the more perishable foods, is purchased from abroad.[100] A great proportion of the funds appropriated for supplies by the Government of India is spent in England.

As early as 1783 Edmund Burke predicted that the annual drain of Indian resources to England without equivalent return would eventually destroy India.[101] From Plassey to Waterloo, fifty-seven years, the drain of India's wealth to England is computed by Brooks Adams at two-and-a-half to five billion dollars.[102] He adds, what Macaulay suggested long ago, that it was this stolen wealth from India which supplied England with free capital for the development of mechanical inventions, and so made possible the Industrial Revolution.[103] In 1901 Dutt estimated that one-half of the net revenues of India flowed annually out of the country, never to return.[104] In 1906 Mr. Hyndman reckoned the drain at $40,000,000 a year. A. J. Wilson valued it at one-tenth of the total annual production of India.[105] Montgomery Martin, estimating the drain at $15,000,000 a year in 1838, calculated that these annual sums, retained and gathering interest in India, would amount in half a century to $40,000,000,000.[106] Though it may seem merely spectacular to juggle such figures, it is highly probable that the total wealth drained from India since 1757, if it had all been left and invested in India, would now amount, at a low rate of interest, to $400,000,000,000. Allow for money reinvested in India, and a sum remains easily equivalent to the difference between the poorest and the richest nations in the world. The same high rate of taxation which has bled India to perhaps a mortal weakness, might have done her no permanent injury if the wealth so taken had all been returned into the economy and circulation of the country; but bodily withdrawn from her as so much of it was, it has acted like a long-continued transfusion of vital blood. "So great an economic drain out of the resources of the land," says Dutt, "would impoverish the most prosperous countries on earth; it has reduced India to a land of famines more frequent, more widespread and more fatal, than any known before in the history of India, or of the world."[107]

Sir Wilfred Scawen Blunt sums it up from the point of view of a true Englishman:

> India's famines have been severer and more frequent, its agricultural poverty has deepened, its rural population has become more hopelessly in debt, their despair more desperate. The system of constantly enhancing the land values (i.e. raising the valuation and assessment) has not been altered. The salt tax . . . still robs the very poor. . . . What was bad twenty-five years ago is worse now. At any rate there is the same drain of India's food to alien mouths. Endemic famines and endemic plagues are facts no official statistics can explain away. . . . Though myself a good Conservative . . . I own to being shocked at the bondage in which the Indian people are held; . . . and I have come to the conclusion that if we go on de-

veloping the country at the present rate, the inhabitants, sooner or later, will have to resort to cannibalism, for there will be nothing left for them to eat.[108]

VI. Social Destruction

From such poverty come ignorance, superstition, disease and death. A people reduced to these straits cannot afford education; they cannot afford the taxes required to maintain adequate schools; they cannot afford to spare their children from productive employment during the years of public instruction; every penny is taken from them that could have been used for proper education.

When the British came there was, throughout India, a system of communal schools, managed by the village communities. The agents of the East India Company destroyed these village communities, and took no steps to replace the schools; even to-day, after a century of effort to restore them, they stand at only 66% of their number a hundred years ago.[109] There are now in India 730,000 villages, and only 162,015 primary schools.[110] Only 7% of the boys and 1½% of the girls receive schooling; i.e., 4% of the whole.[111] Such schools as the Government has established are not free, but exact a tuition fee which, though small to a Western purse, looms large to a family always hovering on the edge of starvation.

We have been told that the country schools do not grow more rapidly because women teachers cannot be found for them; and that these teachers refuse to go because they fear that they will be raped. But women are considerably safer in India than in New York; not to speak of the invariably passive mood of the verb *seduce.* Every student of India knows that the country schools lag behind not for such lurid reasons, but simply because the pay for new teachers is $5 a month, for a trained teacher $5.00 to $6.50 a month, for principals $7-10 a month. Until 1921 the pay for primary school teachers in the Madras Presidency was $24-36 a year.[112] (Some allowance must be made for the lower cost of commodities in India.) The Government spends every year on education eight cents a head;[113] it spends on the army eighty-three cents a head.[114]

In 1911 a Hindu representative, Gokhale, introduced a bill for universal compulsory primary education in India; it was defeated by the British and Government-appointed members. In 1916

Patel introduced a similar bill, which was defeated by the British and Government-appointed members;[115] the Government could not afford to give the people schools. Instead, it spent most of its eight cents for education on secondary schools and universities, where the language used was English, the history, literature, customs and morals taught were English, and young Hindus, after striving amid poverty to prepare themselves for college, found that they had merely let themselves in for a ruthless process that aimed to de-nationalize and de-Indianize them, and turn them into imitative Englishmen. The first charge on a modern state, after the maintenance of public health, is the establishment of education, universal, compulsory and free. But the total expenditure for education in India is less than one-half the educational expenditure in New York State.[116] In the quarter of a century between 1882 and 1907, while public schools were growing all over the world, the appropriation for education in British India increased by $2,000,000; in the same period appropriations for the fratricide army increased by $43,000,000.[117] It pays to be free.

Hence the 93% illiteracy of India. In several provinces literacy was more widespread before the

British took possession than it is now after a century and a half of British control;[118] in several of the states ruled by native princes it is higher than in British India. "The responsibility of the British for India's illiteracy seems to be beyond question."[119] The excuse that caste interferes with education will not hold; caste did not interfere with the crowding of every Hindu class indiscriminately in railway coaches, tram-cars and factories; it need not have interfered with schools; the best way to conquer caste would have been through schools. Is it any wonder that a people so stupefied with poverty and lack of education is too ignorant to use birth-control, and practises superstitions worse even than those of the West?

Instead of encouraging education, the Government encouraged drink. When the British came, India was a sober nation. "The temperance of the people," said Warren Hastings, "is demonstrated in the simplicity of their food and their total abstinence from spirituous liquors and other substances of intoxication."[120] With the first trading-posts established by the British, saloons were opened for the sale of rum, and the East India Company made handsome profits from the trade.[121] When the Crown took over India it depended on the saloons for a large part of its revenue; the license system was so arranged as to stimulate drinking and sales. The Government revenue from such licenses has increased seven-fold in the last forty years; in 1922 it stood at $60,000,000 annually—three times the appropriation for schools and universities.

Miss Mayo tells us that Hindu mothers feed opium to their children; and she concludes that India is not fit for Home Rule. What she says is true; what she does not say makes what she says worse than a straightforward lie. She does not tell us (though she must have known) that women drug their children because the mothers must abandon them every day to go to work in the factories. She does not tell us that the opium is grown only by the Government, and is sold exclusively by the Government; that its sale, like the sale of drink through saloons, is carried on despite the protests of the Nationalist Congress, the Industrial and Social Conferences, the Provincial Conferences, the Brahmo-Somaj, the Arya-Somaj, the Mohammedans and the Christians; that there are seven thousand opium shops in India, operated by the British Government, in the most conspicuous places in every town;[122] that the Central Legislature in 1921 passed a bill prohibiting the growth or sale of opium in India, and that the Government refused to act upon it;[123] that from two to four hundred thousand acres of India's soil, sorely needed for the raising of food, are given over to the growing of opium;[124] and that the sale of the drug brings to the Government one-ninth of its total revenue every year.[125] She does not tell us that Burma excluded opium by law until the British came, and is now overrun with it; that the British distributed it free in Burma to create a demand for it;[126] that whereas the traffic has been stopped in the Philippines, England has refused, at one World Opium Conference after another, to abandon it in India; that though she has agreed to reduce the export of opium by 10% yearly, she has refused to reduce its sale in India; that the Report of the Government Retrenchment Commission of 1925 emphasized "the importance of safeguarding opium sales as an important source of revenue," and recommended "no further reduction";[127] that when Gandhi by a peaceful anti-opium campaign in Assam had reduced the consumption of the drug there by one-half, the Government put a stop to his labors and jailed forty-four of his aides.[128] She does not tell us that the health, courage and character of the Hindu people have been undermined through this ruthless drugging of a nation by men pretending to be Christians.

On July 10, 1833, Lord Macaulay addressed the House of Commons as follows:

> It was . . . the practice of the miserable tyrants whom we found in India, that when they dreaded the capacity and spirit of some distinguished subject, and yet could not venture to murder him, to administer to him a daily dose of the *pousta*, a preparation of opium, the effect of which was in a few months to destroy all the bodily and mental powers of the wretch who was drugged with it, and turn him into a helpless idiot. That detestable artifice, more horrible than assassination itself, was worthy of those who employed it. It is no model for the English nation. We shall never consent to administer the *pousta* to a whole community, to stupefy and paralyze a great people.[129]

These words were spoken almost a century ago.

VII. The Triumph of Death

The last chapter is disease and death.

The emaciation of the Hindus sickens the traveler; closed fingers can be run up around their bare legs from the ankles to the knees. In the cities 34% of them are absent from work, on any day, from illness or injury. They are too poor to afford foods rich in mineral salts; they are too poor to buy fresh vegetables, much less to buy meat. The water-supply, which is usually the first obligation of a government, is in primitive condition, after a century or more of British rule; dysentery and malaria have been eliminated from Panama and Cuba, but they flourish in British India. Once the Hindu was known to be among the cleanest of the clean;[130] and even to-day he bathes every morning, and washes every morning the simple garment that he wears; but the increase of poverty has made social sanitation impossible. Until 1918 the total expenditure on public health, of both the central and the provincial governments combined, was only $5,000,000 a year, for 240,000,000 people—an appropriation of two cents per capita.[131]

Sir William Hunter, once Director-General of Indian Statistics, estimated that 40,000,000 of the people of India were seldom or never able to satisfy their hunger.[132] Weakened with malnutrition, they offer low resistance to infections; epidemics periodically destroy millions of them. In

1901, 272,000 died of plague introduced from abroad; in 1902, 500,000 died of plague; in 1903, 800,000; in 1904, 1,000,000.[133] In 1918 there were 125,000,000 cases of influenza, and 12,500,000 recorded deaths.[134]

We can now understand why there are famines in India. Their cause, in plain terms, is not the absence of sufficient food, but the inability of the people to pay for it. Famines have increased in frequency and severity under British rule. From 1770 to 1900, 25,000,000 Hindus died of starvation; 15,000,000 of these died in the last quarter of the century, in the famines of 1877, 1889, 1897, and 1900.[135] Contemporary students [136] estimate that 8,000,000 will die of starvation in India during the present year. It was hoped that the railways would solve the problem by enabling the rapid transport of food from unaffected to affected regions; the fact that the worst famines have come since the building of the railways proves that the cause has not been the lack of transportation, nor the failure of the monsoon rains (though this, of course, is the occasion), nor even overpopulation (which is a contributory factor); behind all these, as the fundamental source of the terrible famines in India, lies such merciless exploitation, such unbalanced exportation of goods, and such brutal collection of high taxes in the very midst of famine,[137] that the starving peasants cannot pay what is asked for the food that the railways bring them. American charity has often paid for the relief of famine in India while the Government was collecting taxes from the dying. "There has never been a single year," says Dutt, "when the food-supply of the country was insufficient for the people."[138] Let the late President of Union Theological Seminary, Dr. Charles C. Hall, speak:

> The obvious fact stares us in the face that there is at no time, in no year, any shortage of food-stuffs in India. The trouble is that the taxes imposed by the British Government being 50% of the produce, the Indian starves that India's annual revenue may not be diminished by a dollar. 80% of the whole population has been thrown back upon the soil because England's discriminating duties have ruined practically every branch of native manufacture. . . . We send shiploads of grain to India, but there is plenty of grain in India. The trouble is that the people have been ground down till they are too poor to buy it. Famine is chronic there now, though the same shipments of food-stuffs are made annually to England, the same drainage of millions of dollars goes on every year.[139]

The final item is the death-rate. In England the death-rate is 13 per 1000 per year; in the United States it is 12; in India it is 32.[140] Half the children born in Bengal die before reaching the age of eight.[141] In a recent year (1921) the infant mortality in Bombay was 666 per 1000; in one-room tenements it was 828 per 1000.[142] Lt.-Col. Dunn, of the Indian Medical Service, says that one-half of the death-rate is preventable; if we doubt this we need only study the case of Cuba, which under Spanish rule was ridden with malaria, typhus and cholera, and had one of the world's highest death-rates, while now, under freedom, it has become one of the healthiest of countries, and its death-rate is among the lowest known.[143] But in India ten are born that three, or six, or eight of them may die within a year.

This is the conclusion of the play: taxation, exploitation, starvation, death.

And now, having quoted authorities sufficiently to guard against relying on my own too brief experience, I may be permitted, despite that limitation, to express my own judgment and feeling. I came to India admiring the British, marveling at their imperial capacity for establishing order and peace, and thankful for the security which their policing of the world's waters has given to every traveler. I left India feeling that its awful poverty is an unanswerable indictment of its alien government, that so far from being an excuse for British rule, it is overwhelming evidence that the British ownership of India has been a calamity and a crime. For this is quite unlike the Mohammedan domination: those invaders came to stay, and their descendants call India their home; what they took in taxes and tribute they spent in India, developing its industries and resources, adorning its literature and art. If the British had done likewise, India would to-day be a flourishing nation. But the present plunder has now gone on beyond bearing; year by year it is destroying one of the greatest and gentlest peoples of history.

The terrible thing is that this poverty is not a beginning, it is an end; it is not growing less, it is growing worse; England is not "preparing India for self-government," she is bleeding it to death. "Even as we look on," said another loyal Englishman, H. M. Hyndman, "India is becoming feebler and feebler. The very life-blood of the great multitude under our rule is slowly, yet ever faster ebbing away."[144]

Any man who sees this crime, and does not speak out, is a coward. Any Englishman or any American, seeing it and not revolted by it, does not deserve his country or his name.

CHAPTER TWO

GANDHI

I. Portrait

Picture the ugliest, slightest, weakest man in Asia, with face and flesh of bronze, close-cropped gray head, high cheek bones, kindly little brown eyes, a large and almost toothless mouth, larger ears, an enormous nose, thin arms and legs, clad in a loin-cloth, standing before an English judge in India, on trial because he has preached liberty to his countrymen. Picture him again similarly dressed, at the Viceroy's palace in Delhi, in conference on equal terms with the highest representative of England. Or picture him seated on a small carpet in a bare room at his Satyagrahashram, or School of Truth-Seekers, at Ahmedabad; his bony legs crossed under him in Yogi fashion, soles upward, his hands busy at a spinning-wheel, his face lined with the sufferings of his people, his mind active with ready answers to every questioner of freedom. This naked weaver is both the spiritual and the political leader of 320,000,000 Hindus; when he appears in public, crowds gather round him to touch his clothing or to kiss his feet;[1] not since Buddha has India so reverenced any man. He is in all probability the most important, and beyond all doubt the most interesting, figure in the world today. Centuries hence he will be remembered when of his contemporaries hardly a name will survive.

He receives you without effusion or ceremony; for you he provides a chair, but he is content to squat on the floor. He looks at you a moment, smiles his acknowledgment of your interest in India, and resumes his spinning while he talks. Four hours a day he spins the coarse *khaddar*. His only possessions in the world are three *khaddar* cloths, which serve him as a wardrobe; once a rich lawyer, he has given all his property to the poor, and his wife, after some womanly hesitation, has followed his example. He sleeps on a piece of *khaddar* spread on the bare floor or the earth. He lives on nuts, plantains, lemons, oranges, dates, rice and goat's milk;[2] often for months together he takes nothing but milk and fruit; he has tasted meat but once in his life. Usually he eats with the children whom he teaches; they are his sole recreation, and when His Majesty's officers came to arrest him, in 1922, they found him frolicking in the yard with these youngsters. He not only prays, rising at four a.m. for an hour of prayer and meditation, but he fasts. "I can as well do without my eyes," he says, "as without fasts. What the eyes are for the outer world, fasts are for the inner;"[3] as the blood thins, the mind clears, irrelevancies fall away, and fundamental things, sometimes even the Soul of the World, come into vision like mountain-tops through a cloud.

At the same time that he fasts to see God, he keeps one toe on the earth, and advises his followers to take an enema daily when they fast, lest they be poisoned with the acid products of the body's self-consumption just as they are finding God.[4] When, in 1924, the Moslems and the Hindus were engaged in killing one another theologically, and paid no heed to his pleas for peace, he went without food for three weeks to move them. He has become so weak and frail through fasts and privations that when he addresses audiences he must, in most cases, speak from a chair.[5]

He carries his asceticism into the field of sex, and like Tolstoi he would limit all physical intercourse to deliberate reproduction. In his youth he indulged the flesh too much, and the news of his father's death surprised him in the arms of love. He returned with passionate remorse to the Hindu doctrine of *Brahmacharya* which had been preached to him in his youth—absolute abstention from all sensual desire. He persuaded his wife that they should live henceforth like brother and sister, avoiding all sexual behavior; and "from that time," he tells us, "all dissension ceased."[6] When later he realized that India's basic need was birth-control, he adopted not the methods of the West, but the theories of Malthus and Tolstoi.

> Is it right for us, who know the situation, to bring forth children? We only multiply slaves and weaklings if we continue the process of procreation whilst we feel and remain helpless. . . . Not till India has become a free nation . . . have we the right to bring forth progeny. . . . I have not a shadow of doubt that married people, if they wish well to the country and want to see India become a nation of strong and handsome, well-formed men and women, would practise perfect self-restraint and cease to procreate for the time being.[7]

With such a history behind him he is naturally a rigorist in morals. He believes with Christ that he who looks upon a woman with desire in his heart has already committed adultery. He abominates prostitution, and denounces the West for abusing a minority of the "nobler sex" in order to satisfy bachelors and adulterers.[8] Prostitutes have been comforted by his message, and have come great distances to lay their savings at his feet and pledge themselves to continence.[9] He admits that India is over-sexed, and partly for that reason he would welcome the total prohibition of alcoholic beverages in his country.[10] Even art seems to him a vain and frivolous thing when it is divorced from nature and morals.

> I love music and all the other arts, but I do not attach such value to them as is generally done. I cannot, for example, recognize the value of all these activities which require special technical knowledge for their understanding. . . . When I gaze at the star-sown heaven, and the infinite beauty it affords my eyes, that means more to me than all that human art can give me. That does not mean that I ignore the value of those works generally called artistic; but personally, in comparison with the infinite beauty of nature, I feel their unreality too intensely. . . . Life is greater than all art.[11]

Added to these elements in his character, which must make him an unattractive figure to our Epicurean West, are qualities strangely like those that (we are told) distinguished Christ. He does not mouth the name of the Founder of Christianity, but he acts as if the Sermon on the Mount were his perpetual guide. Not since St. Francis of Assisi has any life known to history been so marked by gentleness, disinterestedness, simplicity of soul, and forgiveness of enemies. It is to the credit of his opponents, but still more to his own, that his courtesy to them has been so consistent that it has won from them a fine courtesy in return; the Government sends him to jail with the most profuse apologies. He has never shown rancor or resentment. Three times he has been attacked by mobs, and been beaten almost to death; not once has he retaliated; and when a leading assailant was arrested he refused to make any charge against him. Shortly after the worst of all riots between Moslems and Hindus, when the Mohammedans of Moplah butchered hundreds of unarmed Hindus and offered their prepuces as a covenant to Allah, these same Moplahs were stricken with famine; whereupon Gandhi collected funds for them from all India, and (with no regard for the best precedents in matters of charity) forwarded every *anna*, without deduction for "overhead," to the starving enemy.[12]

Missionaries in India hail him as the greatest

Christian of our time. Like Buddha and Miranda, he has suffered with those he has seen suffer; he has taken all the tribulation of his people upon himself, fighting for their freedom and fasting for their sins. And so a nation that would never have been thrilled by a purely secular call, has put itself trustfully into his hands, has accepted his hard doctrine of peaceful resistance, and has anointed him as its leader and prophet, its *Mahatma*, or Great Soul. We have the astonishing phenomenon of a revolution led by a saint.

II. Preparation

He was born in 1869 at Porbander, in the province of Gujerat, and was named Mohandas Karamchand Gandhi. His family belonged to the Vaisya caste, or business class, and to the Jain sect of religious devotees, who practised the principle of never injuring a living thing. His father was a capable administrator but an unorthodox financier; he lost place after place through honesty, gave nearly all his wealth to charity, and left the rest to his family.[13] Mohandas went to the village school, and increased rapidly in wisdom and understanding. While still a boy he became an atheist, being displeased with the gallantries of certain adulterous Hindu gods; and to make clear his everlasting scorn for religion, he scandalized everyone by eating meat. The meat disagreed with him, and he became religious again.

At eight he was engaged, and at twelve he was married, to Kasturbai, who has been loyal to him through all his adventures, riches, poverty, imprisonments, and *Brahmacharya*. At eighteen he passed examinations for the university, and went to London to study law. His mother was loath to see him go, and exacted from him a promise, sworn to before a priest, to abstain from wine, meat, and sexual relations while away from India.[14] In London he did his best to become an "English gentleman"; he dressed with devotion, and took lessons in elocution, dancing, violin and French.[15] The schedule proved too much for him, and in a lucid interval he threw over the whole social curriculum, and resolved to abandon forever the attempt to be an Englishman. When he returned to India he was more Hindu than before.

Those years in London taught him three subversive ideas: nationalism, democracy, and Christianity. He observed the free life of the English, and their control over their Government; and he conceived the idea that his own people would enjoy a like independence. He admired the English form of government, and wished that British practice would conform with English theory; he marveled that a people so dedicated to liberty should be capable of enslaving a nation. The London Vegetarian Society won him to its creed, and the English Theosophists persuaded him to study the most famous production of his country's literature, the *Bhagavad-Gita.*[16] He read Mazzini, and felt for India all that that passionate patriot had felt for Italy. He read Thoreau, and learned from him the art of civil disobedience; he translated parts of Plato and Ruskin; and he consumed page after page of Tolstoi. Here again was the doctrine of resistance without violence; here too was the condemnation of all non-reproductive sexual relations. In his first year in England he read eighty books on Christianity; but the only one of them that seemed to him to understand Christ was the New Testament. The Sermon on the Mount "went straight to my heart on the first reading."[17] He took the counsels to return good for evil, and to avoid all violence even to enemies, as the highest expression of all human idealism; and he resolved rather to fail with these than to succeed without them.

He had gone to England in 1888; in 1891, having been admitted to the Bar, he returned to India. For a while he practised law in Bombay. He refused to prosecute for debt, and always reserved the right to abandon a case which he had come to think unjust.[18] In 1893 he received a call from South Africa to conduct some litigation for a Hindu firm doing business in Pretoria. When for this second time he left India he thought he would return to it presently and permanently; he did not suspect that Africa would hold him for twenty years. Within a short time after his arrival he had built up for himself a profitable practice in Johannesburg, with an income of over $20,000 a year.[19] He was, for those days, and at a remarkably early age, a rich man.

He found his fellow-Hindus in South Africa bitterly maltreated by prejudice and law. They had come to Natal originally as contract laborers; gradually they had built up a thriving settlement, whose growth gave the English and the Boers an unpleasant topic to agree upon. These practical peoples took various means of suggesting to the Hindus the desirability of their returning to India at an early date: they threw them out of trains and hotels, insulted them, kicked them down stairs, and had them beaten up by those expert gangs which can be hired for these purposes in all civilized communities.[20] In 1906 the South African Government passed an act requiring the Hindus to report to the police for the taking of their thumb-prints. In 1912 the Union Court of South Africa declared all marriages by Hindu rite to be null and void; and the Government of Natal laid upon every Hindu in the province a poll tax of $15 a year.

Gandhi was about to return to India when a committee of Hindus asked his help against these disabilities. They offered him large fees. He agreed to remain and give himself to their cause; he refused all pay, abandoned the comfortable mode of life to which he had become accustomed, and devoted all his time, for the next twenty years, to the cause of his countrymen in Africa. He organized and guided them, taught them peaceful resistance, and built for their refuge a rural retreat where any Hindu might come and live if, like Gandhi, he would take the vows of poverty and non-violence. He presented the case of his people in London, and secured large concessions.

He presented their case in India, and roused the mother country to indignation. When he returned to Africa an enraged mob of white men attacked him at the pier, and he was saved only because an Englishwoman bravely interposed her own body between him and the blows. It was a characteristic example of the English spirit of fair play in a surrounding of British stupidity: the crowd had long before announced its intentions, and an honorable government could easily have dispersed it.

Gandhi himself was not over-consistent in those days. When England fought the Boers he favored England, organized a Red Cross unit of a thousand Hindus, and led them so intrepidly under fire that he was cited for bravery and awarded a medal of honor. He had hoped that a grateful England would repay this loyalty of his race; instead, the concessions promised to him in London were ignored, and when he protested he was sent to jail. The authorities were soon compelled to release him, for the Hindus, freed from his leadership, had reverted to violence. The Government suggested to him that if he would obey the registration law it would remove many of the disabilities affecting the Hindus. He agreed, but on the way to register he was set upon by some Mohammedans among his followers, who, inspired with the thought that he was betraying them, beat him nearly to death. He had himself carried to the place of registry, registered, and fell unconscious. The British arrested the chief assailant, but Gandhi refused to make a complaint against him. "The man will yet be my friend," he said.

His people now followed him in his compromise, and the Government rewarded them with a *promise* to repeal the poll tax. When the promise was not kept, Gandhi led a vast procession of Hindus in protest. He was again arrested, and was sentenced to fifteen months' imprisonment. Finally in 1913 the Government yielded, repealed the poll tax, and restored the validity of Hindu marriage.[21] A year later Gandhi returned to India.

III. Revolution by Peace

Perhaps only now, when he came back to his native country as a mature man, seasoned with experience and tempered with suffering, did he realize the extent of the destitution and slavery of his people. He was horrified, in his sharp social conscience, by the skeletons whom he saw in the fields of India, and the lowly Outcastes in the towns. It dawned upon him that the disabilities of his countrymen abroad were merely one consequence of their poverty and subjection at home. He was moved as Buddha had been by the sight of his fellows' suffering.

> I came reluctantly to the conclusion that the British connection had made India more helpless than she ever was before, politically or economically. . . . The Government established by law in British India is carried on for this exploitation of the masses. No sophistry, no jugglery in figures, can explain away the evidence the skeletons in many villages present to the naked eye. I have no doubt whatsoever that both England and the town-dwellers of India will have to answer, if there is a God above, for this crime against humanity which is perhaps unequalled in history.[22]

At the height of his first non-co-operation movement he offered to the Government to abandon his whole program of resistance to it, and to co-operate with it loyally, if it would undertake an energetic campaign against *starvation* in India.[23] The Government did not see the necessity.

He had hardly established himself at home when the Great War began. That same preference for loyalty and co-operation which had marked him in Africa drove him now to devote his energies and abilities as a leader to helping the cause of Britain in every way but by violence. His naïve confidence in the innocence of the Allies went so far that he advocated the enlistment of Hindus who did not accept the principle of non-violence. He did not, at that time, agree with those who called for the full independence of India; he believed that British misgovernment in India was an exception, and that British government in general was good; that British government in India was bad just because it violated all the principles of British government at home; that if the British people could only be made to understand the case of the Hindus, it would soon accept them in full brotherhood into a commonwealth of free dominions.[24] He trusted that when the War was over, and Britain counted India's sacrifice for the Empire in men and wealth, it would not hesitate any longer to give her liberty. In 1918 he wrote:

> If I could make my countrymen retrace their steps, I would make them withdraw all the Congress resolutions and not whisper "Home Rule" or "responsible government" during the pendency of the War. I would make India offer all her able-bodied sons as a sacrifice to the Empire at its critical moment; and I know that India, by this very act, would become the most favorite partner,

and racial distinctions would become a thing of the past.[25]

At the close of the War the British met the movement for Home Rule by passing the Rowlatt Acts, which put an end to freedom of speech and press; by announcing, through Lord Birkenhead and Lloyd George, that England had no intention of releasing her hold on India; by establishing the impotent legislature of the Montagu-Chelmsford Reforms; and finally, by the massacre of Amritsar.*

Gandhi was horrified. On August 1, 1920, he wrote as follows to the Viceroy:

> It is not without a pang that I return the Kaisar-i-Hind Gold Medal granted to me by your predecessor for my humanitarian work in South Africa; the Zulu War Medal, granted in South Africa for my services as an officer in charge of the Indian Volunteer Ambulance Corps in 1906; and the Boer War Medal for my services as assistant superintendent of the Indian Volunteer Stretcher-Bearer Corps during the Boer War. . . . I can retain neither respect nor affection for a Government which has been moving from wrong to wrong in order to defend its immorality. . . . I have therefore ventured to suggest non-co-operation, which enables those who wish, to dissociate themselves from the

* Cf. Chapter Three.

> Government, and which, if unattended by violence, must compel the Government to retrace its steps and undo its ways.[26]

From his quiet Ashram he sent forth throughout India a call for *Satyagraha*, truth-seeking, truth-gripping; no mere passive resistance, but an active civil disobedience to an unjust government, and a refusal to co-operate with it in any way. He had derived the idea from Thoreau, Tolstoi, and Christ; he had been encouraged in it by his correspondence with Tolstoi, and by the great Russian's "Address to a Hindu"; he had practised it successfully in Africa and in India. In 1918 he had found the peasants of Kaira, in his own province of Gujerat, suffering from oppressive taxation; he had advised them to refuse any taxes at all until the Government should come to reason; they had taken his advice, and borne patiently the punishments inflicted upon them; and they had won.[27]

As offered by him now, *Satyagraha* meant many things: the surrender of all titles and offices held by Hindus under the Government; abstention from all Governmental functions, administrative or social; the gradual withdrawal of Hindu children from Government schools, and the establishment of national schools and colleges to take their place; the withdrawal of Hindu funds from Government bonds; the boycott of Government courts, and the establishment of private arbitration tribunals to settle disputes among Hindus; refusal to perform military service; the boycott of British goods; and the propaganda of *Swaraj*, Self-Rule.[28] Even the protection of the police and the state were to be scorned. "The sooner we cease to rely on Government-protection against one another, the better it will be for us, and the quicker and more lasting will be the solution."[29]

More important than all these details to Gandhi was the method to be used; for without the method the goal would be worthless. Greater than *Satyagraha* was *Ahimsa*, without injury. Unlike the Revolutionists of the West, Gandhi considers no end worth while whose attainment requires violence; the greatest aim of all is to lift man out of the beast; violence is a reversion to the jungle, and the ability to oppose without hating or injuring is the test of the higher man.

This gospel of a loving resistance pleased the Hindus because for two thousand years and more their religions had taught them gentleness and peace. Buddha had counseled them, five centuries before Christ, never to injure any living thing; Mahavira, earlier than Buddha, had instructed his Jain sect likewise; Brahminism had taken over the doctrine, and had made it almost universal in India. Gandhi's family had belonged to just the sect which had set most store on the practice of Ahimsa. Religion seemed to Gandhi more important than politics, and humaneness more than independence; his fundamental conception of religion was reverence for all life. He added to the Hindu form of the principle Christ's doctrine of loving one's enemies; time and again he has pardoned his foes; and in the breadth of his charity he loves even Englishmen.[30]

He is not quite a doctrinaire; he recognizes exceptions. "I believe that where there is only a choice between cowardice and violence, I would advise violence."[31] If a man is peaceful out of fear, Gandhi would rather have him be violent. He says, with characteristic candor and bravery, risking his leadership with a word: "The Hindu, as a rule, is a coward."[32] Certain Hindus allowed robbers to loot their homes and insult their women; he asks: "Why did not the owners of the houses looted die in the attempt to defend their possessions? . . . My non-violence does not admit of running away from danger, and leaving dear ones unprotected."[33] For too many weaklings, he says, non-violence serves merely "as a mask to cover their abject cowardice. . . . Must they not develop the ability to defend themselves violently before they could be expected to appreciate non-violence?"[34] Nevertheless there is in such cases something higher than violent resistance; it is when a man attacked resists as well as he can without violence, and then, overcome, refuses to surrender, but accepts the blows unanswered, and if necessary dies at his post. So it should be with India.

> I would risk violence a thousand times rather than emasculation of the race. I would rather have India resort to arms to defend her honor than that she should in a cowardly manner become or remain a helpless victim to her own dishonor. But I believe that non-violence is infinitely superior to violence.[35]

He distrusts violence because at the outset it empowers the unreasoning mob, and in the end it exalts not the just man but the most violent. He rejects Bolshevism, therefore, as alien to the character and purpose of India. "It may be that in other countries Governments may be overthrown by brute force; but India will never gain her freedom by the naked fist."[36] His newer aides, like the younger Nehru, are eager to arm the Hindus and follow Russia's example; but Gandhi warns them that a freedom based upon killing can never lead to anything more than a change of masters. "I do not believe in short-violent-cuts to success. Bolshevism is the necessary result of modern materialistic civilization. Its insensate worship of matter has given rise to a school which has been brought up to look upon materialistic advancement as the goal, and which has lost all touch with the final things of life."[37]

It is our good fortune, in America, that Lenin and Gandhi do not agree, and that two great peoples, as if for our instruction, are moving by diverse paths to kindred ends. Just as Russia and America are rival laboratories designed, so to speak, by the Spirit of History to test the communistic vs. the individualistic method of production, distribution and living, so Russia and India will be rival laboratories to test the violent vs. the peaceful method of social revolution. Never has history made such crucial experiments on so vast a scale, or offered any generation, not even Christ's, so significant a spectacle. For in India Christ is again on trial, and stands face to face once more with Rome.

But is not non-violent resistance a vain idealist's dream? One hears the sardonic laughter of Lenin. And Gandhi asks in return what progress is made when one form of violence is replaced by another, or materialistic ambition is incorporated and nationalized at the point of a million bayonets? "You of the West," he says, "have been taught it is violent power which wins. The truth is that it is passive resistance which has always won."[38] He cites the victory of the Christians over the Roman Empire as the classic example; and in our own day, he thinks, the League of Nations can re-order the world by practising non-co-operation without violence.[39] He regretted the decision of China to fight the West with the weapons of the West, and predicted that the only result would be a patriotic substitution of home-made violence for foreign. "In casting off Western tyranny it is quite possible for such a nation to become enslaved to Western thought and methods. This second slavery is worse than the first."[40] Always it is better to lose without violence than to win with it: in the one case we sacrifice our personal will (which is a delusion); in the other we sacrifice our distinctive humanity itself.

The West will think *Ahimsa* a weakling's creed, a fig-leaf of philosophy to hide an intellectual's cowardice. Therefore, Gandhi tells his people, India must be ready to suffer anything in its campaign for freedom, and yet never make violent retaliation. To blows and shots, to bombs and shells there must be but one reply: patient refusal to deal in any way with British merchants, British goods, or the British Government. "Bravery on the battlefield is impossible for India, but bravery of the soul remains open to us. Non-co-operation means nothing less than training in self-sacrifice."[41] It is as a brother said to Dhan Gopal Mukerji: "Until our blood is spilt in rivers, nothing can shake the foundation of British rule. . . . We should make a holocaust of ourselves. Even if we are beaten it will cleanse India of cowardice."[42] When Hindus talk like this, freedom is near.

IV. Christ Meets John Bull

We shall tell later the story of the Revolt of 1921: how it made rapid progress in unifying

India with the call to liberty; how it broke out into violence at Bombay and Chauri Chaura; and how Gandhi, in the face of bitter criticism from his followers, withdrew the whole movement on the ground that it was degenerating into mob rule. Seldom in history has a man shown more courage in acting on principle in contempt of passing expediency and popularity. The nation was astonished at his decision; it had supposed itself near to success; and it did not agree with Gandhi that the method was as important as the end. The reputation of the Mahatma sank to the lowest ebb.

It was just at this point (in March, 1922) that the Government, which had feared to touch him before, determined upon his arrest. Charging him with sedition, it sent soldiers to take him into custody. He made no attempt to elude or resist them; he asked his followers to make no protests or demonstrations; and he declined to engage a lawyer or offer a defense. His courtesy to all infected the Court, and the Judge treated him in the finest tradition of English chivalry. The Prosecutor charged him with being responsible, through his literary campaign, for the violence that had marked the outbreak of 1921. Gandhi's reply disturbed every precedent. He said, quietly:

> I wish to endorse all the blame that the learned Advocate-General has thrown on my shoulder in connection with the incidents in Bombay, Madras, and Chauri Chaura. Thinking over these deeply, and sleeping over them night after night, it is impossible for me to dissociate myself from these diabolical crimes. . . . The learned Advocate-General is quite right when he says that as a man of responsibility, a man having received a fair share of education, having had a fair share of experience of this world, I should have known the consequences of every one of my acts. I knew that I was playing with fire, I ran the risk, and if I was set free, I would still do the same. I felt this morning that I would have failed in my duty if I did not say what I say here just now.
>
> I wanted to avoid violence. I want to avoid violence. Non-violence is the first article of my faith. It is also the last article of my creed. But I had to make my choice. I had either to submit to a system which I considered had done an irreparable harm to my country, or incur the risk of the mad fury of my people bursting forth when they understood the truth from my lips. I know that my people have sometimes gone mad. I am deeply sorry for it, and I am therefore here to submit not to a light penalty but to the highest penalty. I do not ask for mercy. I do not plead any extenuating act. I am here, there-

> fore, to invite and cheerfully submit to the highest penalty that can be inflicted upon me for what in law is a deliberate crime and what appears to me to be the highest duty of a citizen. The only course open to you, Judge, is either to resign your post or inflict on me the severest penalty.[43]

The Judge expressed his profound regret that he had to send to jail one whom millions of his countrymen considered "a great patriot and a great leader"; he admitted that even those who differed from Gandhi looked upon him "as a man of high ideals and of noble and even saintly life."[44] Then he sentenced him to six years in prison. Gandhi's son Devandas followed him on trial, freely acknowledged his guilt of sedition, and asked for the maximum penalty.[45]

Missionaries throughout India compared the proceedings to the trial of Jesus. Universally men said that the old question—what the world would do to Jesus should he return to earth—had been clearly answered: it would put him into jail. The English Bishop of Madras spoke without fear and without equivocation: "I frankly confess, although it deeply grieves me to say it, that I see in Mr. Gandhi the patient sufferer for the cause of righteousness and mercy, a truer representative of the crucified Saviour than the men who have thrown him into prison and yet call themselves by the name of Christ."[46]

Gandhi was put under solitary confinement, but he did not complain. "I do not see any of the other prisoners," he wrote, "though I really do not see how my society could do them any harm." But "I feel happy. My nature likes loneliness. I love quietness. And now I have opportunity to engage in studies that I had to neglect in the outside world."[47] He instructed himself sedulously in the writings of Bacon, Carlyle, Ruskin, Emerson, Thoreau and Tolstoi, and solaced long hours with Ben Jonson and Walter Scott. He read and re-read the *Bhagavad-Gita.* He studied Sanskrit, Tamil and Urdu so that he might be able not only to write for scholars but to speak to the multitude. He drew up a detailed schedule of studies for the six years of his imprisonment, and pursued it faithfully till accident intervened. "I used to sit down to my books," he said later, "with the delight of a young man of twenty-four, and forgetting my four and fifty years and my poor health."[48]

Long before the expiration of his sentence he

was stricken with appendicitis. He had often denounced Western medicine as false and worthless; but when the British physician recommended an operation, Gandhi offered no resistance. It was rather the doctor who hesitated. "If you die under my hands," he said, "every Hindu will think I killed you." Gandhi signed a paper absolving him in advance, and the operation proceeded to a successful conclusion. When the patient was strong enough to leave the hospital the Government did not send him back to jail; it released him (February 24, 1924). A vast crowd of his countrymen gathered at the gates of the prison to welcome him, and many kissed his coarse garment as he passed. But he shunned politics and the public eye, pled his weakness and illness, retired to his school at Ahmedabad, and lived there for many years in solitude with his students.

V. The Religion of Gandhi

From that retreat he sent forth, weekly, editorials to his principal mouth-piece, *Young India*. Never has incidental literature been so vital or so absorbing. From these pages we come to know the man across our barriers of traditions and space; and as we read we perceive that he is not only a saint, but also a prophet and a philosopher.

He is first of all a man of religion: i.e., he believes it is better to be good than great, and that right will conquer in the end. "Most religious men I have met are politicians in disguise. I, however, who wear the guise of a politician, am at heart a religious man."[49] He had to be: a politician, even a statesman, could not have united India; India stands for religion, and will follow only a saint. "My patriotism is subservient to my religion," he says.[50] India is great and holy, but greater and holier is truth. To this extent the nationalism vibrating in the Indian Revolution finds no encouragement in the Oriental Rousseau.

Nevertheless, despite his piety, he laughs at the title *Mahatma,* and rejects the idea that he is a saint. "I have no special revelation of God's will. . . . I have no desire to found a sect." He hoped that his arrest would rid India of "the superstition about my possession of supernatural powers."[51] Doubtless other founders of religion protested in the same way; and Gandhi himself protests to no avail. Already peasant cottages show pictures representing him as a reincarnation of Sri-Krishna.[52] A few centuries hence he will be a god.

He is too tolerant to be the conscious founder of a new religion. He is so inclined towards Christianity that his Hindu enemies call him a "Christian in disguise."[53] He is forever quoting phrases from the New Testament; in one page[54] he cites two Christian hymns; he reminds his followers that "not every man who says 'I am a Congressman'" (i.e., a follower of the revolutionary Hindu National Congress) "is such, but only he who does the will of the Congress."[55] The last words of his book on *Ethical Religion* are taken from Christ. He has scandalized orthodox Hindus by requiring the reading of the New Testament in his school.[56] He accepts Christianity as a moral doctrine, and finds no fundamental anomaly in making it the policy of "heathen" India against "Christian" England. "Why," he asks, "should you self-styled whites get it into your heads that Christianity is your special largess to distribute or interpret? You have made a mess of it yourselves. As a matter of fact, Christ was originally an Asiatic, as were all founders of religion, and I think we understand him much better than you do."[57]

But just as a Hindu can be a Buddhist and a Brahminist, or a Buddhist and an atheist, at the same time, and just as a Chinese can be at once a Confucian, a Taoist and a Buddhist, so Gandhi thinks it nothing strange that he should be at once a Christian and a follower of the ancient Hindu faith. "The world, and therefore we, can no more do without the teaching of Jesus than we can without that of Mohammed or the Upanishads. I hold all these to be complementary of one another, in no case exclusive."[58] "The spirit of the Sermon on the Mount competes almost on equal terms with the *Bhagavad-Gita* for the domination of my heart."[59] He quotes the Golden Rule, and then compares it with a couplet from an old Hindu poem taught him in his childhood: "If a man gives you a drink of water, and you give him a drink in return, that is nothing. Real beauty consists in doing good against evil."[60]

And yet, with all his welcome to Christianity, and his co-operation with Mohammedans, he remains a Hindu in faith as well as in nature and philosophy. "I do not believe," he says bravely, "in the exclusive divinity of the *Vedas*. I believe the *Bible*, the *Koran* and the *Zendavesta* to be as divinely inspired as the *Vedas*."[61] But "nothing elates me so as the music of the *Gita*, or the *Ramayana* of Tulsidas."[62] Christianity is, in general, as true as Hinduism; but "Hinduism tells everyone to worship God according to his own faith or *Dharma*, and so it lives in peace with all religions."[63] For him personally the religion of his own people is best. "My faith offers me all that is necessary for my inner development, for it teaches me to pray. But I also pray that everyone else may develop to the fulness of his being in his own religion, that the Christian may become a better Christian, and the Mohammedan a better Mohammedan. I am convinced that God will one day ask us only what we are and what we do, not the name we give to our being and doing."[64]

He has unequivocally applied this principle of tolerance in action. For India, like America, has its religious divisions, its Catholics called Hindus and its Protestants called Mohammedans. Gandhi has collaborated with the Moslem leaders in their own program, and in a combined program for *Swaraj*; he has presided at Mohammedan Congresses, as Mohammedans have presided at the All-India National Congress; he has worked incessantly to reduce the conflicts between the two groups; he has even endangered his life by a twenty-one-day fast to force Hindu and Moslem leaders to co-operation and peace. He has denounced Hindu hatred of Islam, and Hindu music played in processions before Moslem mosques;[65] he has condemned, at great cost to his popularity, the war of Hindu and Moslem periodicals in the Punjab as "simply scurrilous";[66] and though he has expressed his suspicion that the Government secretly encourages these divisions, he challenges his own followers by telling them that "only those can be set by the ears by a third party who are in the habit of quarreling" of themselves.[67] He carries his confidence in the Moslems to the extent of suggesting that they, like the Christians in India, and the Sikhs, and the Parsees, be allowed to write into the proposed Constitution of an autonomous India their own reservations for the protection of their minorities.[68] Until Moslems and Hindus can agree, he says, all talk of self-rule is idle.[69] He paraphrases the saying of an Englishman, and writes: "If we Indians could only spit in unison, we would form a puddle big enough to drown 300,000 Englishmen."[70] "Hindu-Moslem unity," he preaches tirelessly, "means *Swaraj.*"[71]

There are few things in recent Hindu history more remarkable than Gandhi's announcement of September 18, 1924, referring to the Hindu-Moslem riots at Lucknow.

> The recent events have proved unbearable for me. My helplessness is still more unbearable. My religion teaches me that whenever there is distress which one cannot remove, one must fast and pray. I have done so in connection with my own dearest ones. Nothing, evidently, that I say or write can bring the two communities together. I am therefore imposing on myself a fast of twenty-one days, commencing from today.[72]

Was it a mere piece of display? To a certain extent display was necessary; the need of Hindu-Moslem unity had to be dramatized; an almost theatrical stimulus had to be given to the national consciousness. Therefore Gandhi went, for the period of his fast, to the home of a Mohammedan friend, Maulana Mohamad Ali. For three weeks he lay quietly in bed, taking nothing but water. "I am not aware," he wrote later, "of having suffered any pangs of hunger during the whole of the fast."[73] On the twenty-sixth day leaders from both the hostile camps met at his bedside, and issued the following statement:

> The leaders here present are profoundly moved. . . . We empower the President (of the Conference) personally to communicate to Mahatma Gandhi the solemn resolution of all those taking part, to preserve peace; and to announce to him our unanimous desire that

> he should break his fast immediately. . . . He himself shall select the means to be used to check the spread of the existing evil as rapidly and effectively as possible.[74]

Just as Gandhi is not shocked by Western worship of the Virgin, or the symbolism of the Lamb, or the drama of the Mass, so we must not be shocked at his simple acceptance of certain elements in Hinduism which seem to us rank superstition. As John Haynes Holmes says, "Hinduism belongs to Gandhi as the Judaism of the first century belonged to Jesus."[75] Most disturbing of all these local vestiges is his acceptance of caste. The many minor or subordinate castes which have formed in India will, he believes, soon disappear; but the four fundamental castes will remain, in their present or an equivalent form, because, he thinks, they are demanded by the natural variety and inheritance of ability and character.[76] He does not approve of intermarriage among these groups. To an American who questioned caste he said: "Do you not believe in heredity? Do you not believe in eugenics? Do you not have classes in your country?"[77] And to the complaint that it seemed unjust to hold a capable man through life to a low caste into which he had been born, he replied that he believed in re-incarnation, and therefore relied upon successive *avatars* to redress the balance: A capable Sudra, if he lived honorably, would be re-born into a higher caste.[78] Having offended the radicals and the Westerners with this defense of a dying institution he offends the conservatives, and the great majority of his countrymen, by advocating the emancipation of woman, the elimination of the disabilities affecting widows, the abolition of child-marriage, and above all the removal of "untouchability."[79]

> In the history of the world religions there is perhaps nothing like our treatment of the suppressed classes.[80] If the Indians have become the Pariahs of the Empire, it is retributive justice, meted out to us by a just God. . . . Should we Hindus not wash our blood-stained hands before we ask the English to wash theirs? Untouchability has degraded us, made us Pariahs in South Africa, East Africa, Canada. So long as Hindus wilfully regard Untouchability as part of their religion, so long *Swaraj* is impossible of attainment. India is guilty. England has done nothing blacker.[81]

So he announces, boldly, that self-rule is out of the question, and undeserved, while Untouchability remains. "There is nothing untouchable in humanity."[82] He has adopted an Untouchable girl as his own, a laughing little imp whose gay prattle now rules his home.[83] And to the Untouchables he offers the encouragement of his uncompromising program: "You must have the right of worship in any Temple. . . . You must have admission to schools along with the children of other castes, without any distinction. You must be eligible to the highest office in the land, not excluding even that of the Viceroy. That is my definition of the removal of Untouchability."[84]

Let us face to the full the unpleasant elements in Gandhi's creed. He condones idol-worship as a forgivable aid to the imagination of a people too harassed with poverty to have time for education; and he accepts cordially the Hindu reverence for the cow.

> The cow to me means the entire sub-human world. Man through the cow is enjoined to realize his identity with all that lives. Why the cow was selected for apotheosis is obvious to me. The cow in India was the best companion. She was the giver of plenty. Not only did she give milk, but she also made agriculture possible. This gentle animal is a poem of pity. Protection of the cow means the protection of the whole dumb creation of God.

> . . . Cow-protection is the gift of Hinduism to the world.[85]

And then, with his characteristic courage, he turns once more upon his own people mercilessly. "Cow-protection should commence with ourselves. In no part of the world are cattle worse treated than in India. I have wept to see Hindu drivers goading their oxen with the iron points of their cruel sticks. The half-starved condition of the majority of our cattle is a disgrace to us."[86]

Obviously he accepts cow-protection, or the refusal to kill cattle, as bound up with *Ahimsa*—non-injury to any sentient thing. This is to Gandhi the basic idea of Hinduism, and of all religions;[87] without it religion is merely a holy war. "The die is cast for me. . . . The Hindu must cultivate either of these two—faith in God or faith in one's physical might."[88] *Ahimsa* requires belief in God; for only if the universe is governed by Right—even though a Right which we in our caves cannot understand—can we believe, in the face of violence on the throne, that justice will win at last. In the end we are all actors in the drama which God has composed; we are to God what the characters in Shakespeare's plays were to the mind that created them. "I believe in the absolute oneness of

God, and therefore also of humanity. What though we have many bodies? We have but one soul."[89]

VI. Gandhi's Social Philosophy

It is evident that the profane secularization which industry has brought to the West has not yet affected India; the typical Hindu still thinks in terms of God, while the typical white man thinks in terms of earthly profit and loss. Gandhi would not subscribe to the contention of the Chinese philosopher, Hu Shih, that it is the West which is idealistic, and the East which is materialistic; that saving people from poverty is as spiritual a business as the intellectual love of God. (This phrase of Spinoza's is almost a summary of Hindu philosophy.) Gandhi is not prepared, like Hu Shih, to welcome industrialization, factories, railroads, armies as a necessary price for Oriental liberation from the West. On the contrary he abhors Western civilization; he wishes to be free not only from England, but from that whole life of feverish industry, in office and factory, which England was the first to invent. He looks at the slums and militarism of Japan, and turns aside: India must not go that way. He wonders what is the purpose and fruit of this Western bustle and "overproduction," this strange mechanism for concentrating wealth, in which the rapid production of goods leads to universal depression and poverty; this marvelous system whereby the progress of invention results in great fortunes among a few, and increasing unemployment among the rest. He believes that under this mode of life leisure is destroyed, rivalry takes merely material forms of possession, expenditure and display, and happiness is in the end no greater than before all the inventions and all the wealth.[90] He writes:

> The people of Europe today live in better-built houses than they did a hundred years ago. Formerly they wore skins, and used, as their weapons, spears. Now they wear long trousers, . . . and instead of spears they carry with them revolvers containing five or more chambers. . . . Formerly, when people wanted to fight with one another, they measured between them their bodily strength; now it is possible to take away thousands of lives by one man working behind a gun from a hill.[91]

This is in our day an old point, but to Gandhi it is a living horror. He has seen the worst forms of imperialistic exploitation in South Africa and India, and he has known at first hand the filth and terror of war. For the pursuit of material goods for their own sake inevitably ends in war; our neighbor has something which would suit us well —diamond mines in Africa, coal and iron mines in Europe, oil-wells in Mesopotamia, markets and soil in Asia and South America for our surplus of goods and men; sooner or later we take what we can, and hold what we take; presently it is ours by sacred tradition, and any attempt to put an end to the theft is a violation of the peace of the world. What nobility can there be in a civilization that moves so naturally to murder and suicide, to diplomatic lies and invented atrocities, to universal conscription and a prostituted press, to gigantic national debts, and another war as soon as a new generation of simpletons grows up to believe new lies, not remembering the old? Such a civilization cannot survive; it will die in the next war, which will be between Europe and America. The time will come when the West will ask itself, amid the ruins, "What have we done?"[92]

In these errors of life-perspective the fundamental, which vitiates Western thought throughout, is, to Gandhi, a false conception of education. Every year the West flings upon life a million or more graduates trained in cultural studies or business methods, but utterly untrained in morality and honor. Even if they are taught the Ten Commandments in school, they see with their eyes, out of school, how well one may get along, materially, without these *Verbotens*; soon they are added to the welter of unscrupulous individuals seeking wealth; and when they take public office they make official life a running sore of negligence and corruption.

Gandhi's own school, the *Satyagrahashram*, aims on the contrary at character first and intellect afterward; *Ashram* is a place of discipline, *Satya graha* is the grasping of truth. The teachers vow themselves to absolute veracity, to hurt no living thing, to refrain from sensual desire, to live frugally, to use no manufactured goods from abroad, to take for themselves nothing which they might do without; and the pupils are expected to learn from their example. The course for all includes manual training, spinning, agriculture, and the sharing of every menial task. For ten years the students are taught and fed without charge; then they take the vows of the teacher, or go free into life as the seed-carriers of a higher civilization, pledged only to *Ahimsa*—non-violence to life. Gandhi trusts that such *Ashrams* will arise everywhere in India, rescuing Hindu youth from the de-Hinduizing processes of the Government schools, and creating a people with those qualities of character out of which all good things must come,[93] and without which India may be clever and "enlightened," but never again great.

Hardest of all to understand is Gandhi's rejection of Western medical science. At first, he tells us, he honored the physician, who held himself always ready to alleviate pain. But then he decided that medicine was the art of helping one organ at the expense of another, that it removed effects instead of causes, and that it generated new ills for every one it healed. Like Plato, he would have the sufferer bear his pain, keep the doctor away, and help nature to undertake the cure. It was vivisection that repelled him; he brands it as "man's blackest crime," and says: "I detest the unpardonable slaughter of innocent life in the name of science and humanity so-called; and all the scientific discoveries stained with innocent blood I count as of no consequence." All this vast *pharmacopœa* is unnecessary; let men have fresh air, good water and exercise, and eat only what grows out of the earth, and the doctors will starve.

In Utopia there will be no doctors, just as there will be no railways, no factories, and no slums.[94]

This hostility to everything Western culminates in the rejection of modern industry. The old domestic industry, where peasant men and women plied the spinning wheel and the loom, and kept themselves productively busy in the winter months, was good; but the confinement of men and women in factories, making with machines owned by others fractions of articles whose finished form they will never see, appears to Gandhi a roundabout way of burying humanity in a pyramid of shoddy goods.[95] Most machine products, he believes, are unnecessary; the labor saved in using them is consumed in making and repairing them; if labor is really saved, it is of no benefit to labor, but only to capital; labor is thrown into a panic eloquently named "technological unemployment."[96]

> Machinery is like a snake-hole, which may contain from one to one hundred snakes. . . . Where there is machinery there are large cities, and where there are large cities there are tram-cars. . . . As long as we cannot make pins without machinery, so long will we do without them. The tinsel splendor of glassware we will have nothing to do with, and we will make wicks, as of old, with home-grown

cotton, and use hand-made earthen saucers for lamps.[97]

And then the most romantic passage of all:

> Man is so made by nature as to require him to restrict his movements as far as his hands and feet will take him. . . . Railways are a most dangerous institution. Man by their means is getting farther and farther away from his maker. . . . What is the good of covering great stretches of ground at high speed?[98]

Or, as an anonymous Hindu expresses it to an Englishman: "You have taught us to fly in the air like birds, and to swim in the sea like fishes; but how to live on the earth you do not yet know."[99] What *entrepreneur* will solve that little problem for us?

Gandhi offers a solution.

> What may be hoped for is that Europe, on account of her fine and scientific intellect, will realize the obvious and retrace her steps; and from this demoralizing industrialism she will find a way out. It will not necessarily be a return to the old absolute simplicity. But it will have to be a re-organization in which village life will predominate, and in which brute and material force will be subordinated to spiritual force.[100]

The first move towards this end, he thinks, is the restoration of the spinning wheel. "We must gradually return to the old simplicity!"[101] What joy there is in working with our hands!—what music in the song of the wheel!—how many composers have heard in its humming revolutions the spirit of the earth! "The four hours I devote to this work are more important to me than all the others. The fruits of my labor lie before my eyes."[102] But more than that; for a hundred years now, since English manufactures destroyed the domestic industries of India, the peasant's cottage has been idle in the winter days; for half the year 80% of the Hindus are unemployed through no fault of their own.[103] How well it would be for happiness and a modest prosperity, if the *Charka* could be restored to those homes, filling them with busyness and adding to the pitifully small income of the rural family!

But this revival requires a protective tariff; the spinning wheel cannot compete with the British machine loom; British cloth must be kept out that Hindu *khaddar* may find a sale. Since this is impossible, because of British control of Hindu tariffs and ports, the only recourse left to India is a voluntary boycott of all foreign cloth. In this way

$200,000,000 would be saved to India every year.[104]

So Gandhi renewed the *Swadeshi* movement of the old reformer Tilak; self-production was to be added to *Swaraj*, self-rule. He made the spinning of the *Charka* a test of membership in the National Congress; he asked that every Hindu, even the richest, should wear *khaddar*; if they would do that it would give them unity, and prove them ready to stand together against foreign domination.

The response was not universal—how could it be? The great mass of the Hindu people cannot read; it is hard to reach them. But by 1928 great progress had been made. The spinners' association founded by Gandhi had 166 production depots, and 245 sales depots, taking in $1,250,000 a year;[105] Hindu students everywhere dressed in *khaddar*; distinguished ladies abandoned their Japanese silk *saris* for coarse cloths woven by themselves; prostitutes in brothels and convicts in prison began to spin; and in many cities great feasts of the vanities were arranged, as in Savonarola's day, at which wealthy Hindus and great merchants brought from their homes and warehouses all their imported cloth, and flung them into the fire. In one day at Bombay alone, 150,000 pieces were consumed by the flames.[106] Sceptics complained; but the imagination of India had been aroused; the needed symbol had come.

VII. Criticism

The outstanding feature of this social philosophy, to a Western mind, is its typical resemblance to the romanticism of Rousseau and the "Young Germany" of Schlegel's days. There is the same resentment against "civilization," cities and industries; the same longings for old idealized medieval ways;[107] the same preference for the East as against the West, like the Slavophilism of Dostoievski; the same zealous nationalism and horror of foreign things; the same enthusiasm for vernacular languages, the same revival of early literature;[108] the same call for freedom, based upon the same belief in the natural goodness of men. "I believe in human nature," says Gandhi.[109] And like every romantic rebel he enlarges his own cause to make it the cause of humanity; through India he will liberate the world. "*Swaraj,* Home Rule, is not really our goal. Our battle is really a spiritual battle. . . . We, the miserable outcastes of the Orient, we must conquer freedom for all humanity."[110] When the West is sick to the heart of its "progress" and its prosperity, its machines and its speed, it will turn to India to be saved.

We must not suppose, however, that all the leaders of Hindu thought accept Gandhi's creed. The most interesting pages of his weekly, *Young India,* are those in which Hindus of every rank, from Tagore to the Untouchables, write to him, question his views, and force him often to a precarious defense. When these critics are finished, hardly anything remains for a Westerner to add.

They attack his religion. They consider him not a Hindu but a Christian; they quote his favorite book, the *Bhagavad-Gita,* to show him that Hinduism counsels not non-violence but active striking, "natural killing," for a good cause. At the Delhi Conference a Hindu rose and said: "I oppose this non-violence, this non-co-operation. I ask you, is it Hindu teaching? It is not. Is it Mohammedan teaching? It is not. I will tell you what it is. It is Christian."[111]

They attack his pacifism; lusty young revolutionists call him a coward; politicians call him a missionary; a thousand letters denounce his "non-violence" as playing into the hands of an England that respects (as the Irish Revolution shows) only bombs and guns.[112] Politics, one writer tells him, is no field for saints; it is that everlasting struggle of group with group which is the human correlate of the biological struggle of species with species; and like that, it is part of the inescapable essence of life. Gandhi has remembered Christianity and forgotten Darwin; but life is Darwinian, not Christian. Individuals must compete, groups must compete, nations, alliances must compete; to reduce competition in one of these is to increase it in the others; "conflict is the father of all things." To this traditional pacifism, this turning away from the competitive nature of existence, one critic traces the long subjection and abasement of India. "If we look back," he says, "we discover that foreign dominion over India is a terrible revenge on the country, a revenge which life has taken on a nation which tried to deny life."[113] Meanwhile the younger Nehru pours into the blood of India the iron of his uncompromising creed—revolution without violence if possible, with violence if necessary. If the present pacific movement fails, without doubt violence will come.

Another twits Gandhi with dietetic inconsistencies; if *Ahimsa* means non-violence to any living thing, is it not sinned against in the plucking of any plant, in the eating of any vegetable food?[114] The discovery by the Hindu physicist, Sir Jagadis Chandra Bose, that plants have a sensory system, leaves the religious Hindu in a precarious dietetic condition; how can he live without taking life? Although thousands of Hindus are killed in every year by snake-bites, Gandhi prohibits the killing of serpents. "Let us never forget," he says, "that the serpents have been created by the same God who created us and all other creatures. . . . Thousands of Yogis and Fakirs live in the forests of Hindustan amidst lions, tigers and serpents, but we never hear of their meeting death at the hands of these animals. . . . I have implicit faith in the doctrine that so long as man is not inimical to the other creatures, they will not be inimical to him."[115]

Merciless, his correspondents inform him that *Ahimsa* is especially unsuited to India, because the Hindus, as he admits, are cowards, and will use the doctrine as a cover, while the Mohammedans among the population are natural fighters, whose religion sanctifies killing for a holy cause, and finds many causes holy. "The *Ahimsa* doctrine," says one, "has made us sneaking, sniveling cowards."[116] "Don't you think," asks another, "that armed and conspired resistance against something Satanic and ignoble is infinitely more befitting for any nation . . . than the prevalence of effortlessness and philosophical cowardice? I mean the cowardice which is pervading the length and breadth of India owing to the preaching of your theory of non-violence."[117] "Two years ago," Gandhi writes, "a Mussulman friend said to me in all sincerity: 'I do not believe your non-violence. . . . Violence is the law of life. I would not have *Swaraj* by non-violence. . . . I must hate my enemy.' This friend," adds Gandhi, "is an honest man. I entertain great regard for him."[118]

The critics proceed to point out the difficulties of *Satyagraha*, non-co-operation. First, as regards the masses, they cannot be kept non-violent; aroused as they must be to achieve anything, they will soon smash and kill. Second, as regards Hindu holders of office under the British *Raj*, non-co-operation, by demanding that they resign, puts too heavy a strain on human nature; many who did resign in the first flush of enthusiasm or display have crept back to their sinecures;[119] and hundreds of leading Hindus, who might have supported the demand for Home Rule, are alienated by the call for their resignations—i.e., for what they consider the starvation of their families.[120] So with the boycott of Government schools: teachers who left them are now destitute, and wish they could return; pupils who left them are flocking back. The national schools organized to teach non-co-operating students had no funds, and could purchase only the most primitive equipment and the most depressing quarters; in one town with two Government high schools each having five hundred pupils, the one National high school has fifty.[121] The national schools that sprang up in 1921, have, with few exceptions, died.[122] The boycott of the courts has proved impracticable: e.g., what could be done when officials of the National Congress absconded with Congress funds? To which Gandhi gives reply: "At the risk of being considered inconsistent, I have no hesitation whatsoever in advising the Congress officials in Orissa to take legal proceedings against the culprits for the recovery of trust funds. . . . The Congress has a perfect right to break its own law in its own favor. In a well-ordered state the maxim, 'The King can do no wrong,' has a legitimate purpose and place."[123] It is the strangest passage in *Young India.*

Above all, the critics ridicule his hostility to machinery. "The whole world," says one, "is advancing in material civilization, without which we shall certainly be handicapped. It is now a settled fact that India fell a prey to Western nations because she was wanting in scientific and material progress. History has taught this lesson, and it cannot be overlooked."[124] Sankara Nair, Gandhi's bitterest Hindu opponent, reminds him again and again that partial industrialization is indispensable to the freedom of India, because freedom requires the capacity for self-defense, and self-defense requires wealth.[125] Gandhi answers that he is not against machinery as such—that the spinning-wheel is itself a machine; but he is "a determined foe of all machinery that is designed for the exploitation of people."[126] Meanwhile fact moves on with no regard for argument: new factories spring up every week in Bombay, Calcutta, Ahmedabad and Madras; the Tata Brothers, Hindus, organize one of the greatest iron companies in the world; electric lights, trolley-cars, railways, motor-cars, hotels, warehouses, daily transform the scene; and the traveler observes that the Hindus, just emerging though they are from the Middle Ages, drive automobiles as competently as though they had been raised in Detroit.

Therefore Gandhi's critics laugh at the spinning-wheel, as a vain attempt to turn time back in its flight. It will revolve for a while, by the power of enthusiasm, poetry and imagination, but never can the *Charka* compete with the machine; sooner or later even pious Hindus will buy cloth where it is cheapest and best. The younger reformers think no longer of the *Charka*, but of a protective tariff that will promote the development of factory industry in India. Life inevitably moves out of the village into the city. The first flush of native wealth will put an end to the mysticism of *khaddar*. "*Khaddar* is dearer than mill cloth," writes one correspondent to Gandhi, "and our means are poor."[127] "The mill-owners," another informs him, "do not hesitate to palm off fraudulent imitations of *khaddar* on the gullible public."[128] To which Gandhi answers: "I would ask sceptics to go to the many poor homes where the spinning-wheel is again supplementing their slender resources, and ask the inmates whether the spinning-wheel has not brought joy to their homes."[129]

Finally the poet-sage of India, Rabindranath Tagore, expresses in his gentle way certain difficulties which he finds in the program of his friend. A courteous rivalry has arisen between the *Satyagrahashram* at Ahmedabad, and Tagore's school, *Santiniketan*, at Calcutta. The poet speaks always with the greatest respect of the saint, but always with careful reservations. He finds a note of narrow nationalism in Gandhi; and worse, an unmistakable quality of medieval reaction. "Spin and weave!—is this the gospel of a new creative age?" To hug the *Charka* to oneself, and try to step out of the universal industrializing current of the world, to think that a people can become great by going backward to primitive conditions irrelevant to modern life—this again is a narrow vision. India must move with the age, she must think not in terms of her own oppressed people, but in terms of the oppressed of every nation. To attempt to divide India from the West is spiritual suicide.[130] To which Gandhi replies:

> When all about me are dying for want of food, the only occupation permissible for me is to feed the hungry. . . . To a people famishing and idle, the only acceptable form in which God can dare appear is work, and promise of food as wages. . . . Everyone must spin. Let Tagore spin like the others. Let him burn his foreign cloths. That is the

duty today. God will take care of the tomorrow.[131]

Nothing is more admirable in Gandhi than his conscientious printing of these criticisms in his own press, and his patient and courteous reply to all of them except Tagore's. He knows that he is but human; there is no nonsense of inspiration about him; he says, disarmingly: "Even if my belief is a fond delusion, it will be admitted that it is a fascinating delusion."[132]

And yet, he hopes, it is not a delusion. It is not a nationalist dream: it abhors war and aggrandizement, and trusts to establish a mode of life in which the West, weary of haste, may find something worthy of imitation; it envisages not India only as unhappy and oppressed, but all mankind. He knows that non-co-operation is an imperfect thing, that the ideal would be to co-operate with all; but today it is a necessary discipline, forging into unity the scattered races and villages of India; already it has awakened India from torpor and given it new strength.[133] He knows how frail a weapon of the spirit non-violence is in a world bristling with guns; but what other course is open to a country absolutely weaponless? "You know that we are powerless," he writes in an *Open Let-*

ter to All Englishmen in India, "for you have ensured our incapacity to fight in open and honorable battle."[184] That is a strange phrase for Gandhi! "The British," he writes, "want us to put the struggle on the plane of machine-guns. They have these weapons and we have not. Our only assurance of beating them is to keep it on the plane where we have the weapons and they have not. . . . The way of the sword is not open to India."[135] Yes, violence is the law of the animal world, but it is not the law of the human world; more and more the strength of the spirit outweighs the power of fists and guns.[136] *Ahimsa* may make cowards, or offer them a philosophy of escape; but also it makes saints of limitless bravery, who stand up to the pikes and pistols of the oppressor without fear and without retreat. Let the history of the Revolution prove it! And if India cannot attain freedom without violence, she will not, in the judgment of Gandhi, attain it with violence.

> History teaches one that those who have, no doubt with honest motives, ousted the greedy by using brute force against them, have in their turn become a prey to the disease of the conquered. . . . My interest in India's freedom will cease if she adopts vio-

lent means. For their fruit will be not freedom, but slavery.[137]

VIII. *An Estimate*

How does the man appear now, in the perspective of these examples of his thought? Of course he is above all an idealist, not a realist. He makes very little application of history to the understanding of the present; he is unaware of the careless regularity with which fate has trampled Right under Might, and Beauty under Power; his citation of the Christian conquest of Rome as an instance of successful non-violent non-co-operation ignores the political and economic factors in that "conversion" of Constantine which determined the victory of the Church. The biological view of life is unknown to him; he does not realize that morals and co-operation have been developed only to give a group coherence and strength against competing groups. His theory of the spinning-wheel indicates an over-simplification of this complex and interdependent economic world; no nation can now remain medieval and be free.

Having made this obeisance to reality, we are free to accept and honor Gandhi for his astonishing record of achievements. First, though leaping far ahead of the moral consciousness of mankind, which is yet tribal and national, he has helped the international organization of industries and states to prepare us for the larger morality, in which the code of conduct between gentlemen will be—because world order will necessitate it—applied to the conduct of nations. Second, he has given life and meaning to a Christianity which had become, among ourselves, mere poetry and pretense; he has lifted it up to a plane where the most unscrupulous statesman must reckon with it as a great force; he has ennobled it beyond modern precedent by unconsciously attaching to its banner one-fifth of the human race. Third, he has for a generation kept a great revolutionary movement from all but sporadic violence; he has refused to unleash the mob; in this way he has been a boon to all humanity, which is so sensitive now to disorder anywhere. He has approached one of the fundamental principles of statesmanship: to persuade radicals that change must be gradual in order to be permanent, and to persuade conservatives that change must be. Fourth, he has educated his people: he has aroused them, as no man before in their history, to the evils of Untouchability, temple prostitution, child-marriage, unmarriageable widows, and the traffic in opium. Fifth, and despite his partial defense of that caste system which perpetually divides and weakens India, he has, by the power of imagination and the word, given to India a psychological unity never possessed by it before, making all these races, languages and creeds feel and think alike, as the prelude to united action. Sixth, he has given to his countrymen what they needed above everything else—pride. They are no longer hopeless or supine; they are prepared for danger and responsibility, and therefore for freedom.

If his way of thought seems alien to our sceptical and realistic West, let us remember that our way of thought would be maladapted and useless to the Hindus. The unifier of India could not be a politician, he had to be a saint. Because Gandhi thought with his heart all India has followed him. Three hundred million people do him reverence, and no man in the world wields so great a spiritual influence. It is as Tagore said of him:

> He stopped at the thresholds of the huts of the thousands of dispossessed, dressed like one of their own. He spoke to them in their own language. Here was living truth at last, and not only quotations from books. For this

> reason the "Mahatma," the name given to him by the people of India, is his real name. Who else has felt like him that all Indians are his own flesh and blood? . . . When love came to the door of India that door was opened wide. . . . At Gandhi's call India blossomed forth to new greatness, just as once before, in earlier times, when Buddha proclaimed the truth of fellow-feeling and compassion among all living creatures.[138]

Perhaps Gandhi will fail, as saints are like to fail in this very Darwinian world. But how could we accept life if it did not, now and then, fling into the face of our successes some failure like this?

CHAPTER THREE

THE REVOLUTION

I. Origins

It was Woodrow Wilson who started the Indian Revolution. Did he know what he was doing when he scattered over every land his ringing phrases about democracy, self-government, and the rights of small nations? In every subject country—in Egypt and the Near East, in China and India—there were ears waiting for those words as the signal to revolt. They were the voice of the *Zeitgeist* calling to all men to be free. Were not the Allies winning, and destroying the last autocracy in Europe? Was not the whole world now safe for democracy?

Those waiting spirits, of course, had been prepared; the ideology of liberty was not born in them over night. Young Chinese, young Japanese, young Hindus had gone to Oxford and Cambridge, to London and Manchester, to Harvard and Columbia, to Princeton and Yale. In 1923 there were 1094 Hindu students enrolled in the schools of

England.[1] They marveled at the privileges enjoyed by the lowliest citizens of Europe and America; they studied the French and American Revolutions, and read the liberal literature of reform, the radical literature of revolt; they gloated over the Bill of Rights, The Declaration of the Rights of Man, the Declaration of Independence, and the American Constitution; they went back to their countries as centers of infection for democratic ideas and the gospel of liberty. The industrial and scientific advances of the West, and the victory of the Allies in the War, gave to these ideas an irresistible prestige; soon every student was shouting the battle-cry of freedom. In the schools of England and America the Hindus learned to be free.

And did Macaulay foresee, when he ordained that all higher education in India should use the English language, that the Hindus would learn nationalism and democracy with English? If all great literature, as Thomas Hardy said, is the voice of reason in revolt, how could the young Hindu read the literature of England and America without being corrupted and exalted with the aspiration to freedom? At last the English in India, seeing the mischief that was brewing, forbade the teaching of European history of the eighteenth century in the Indian schools. But they had waited too long.[2]

These Western-educated Orientals had not only taken on political ideas in the course of their education abroad; they had shed religious ideas; the two processes are usually associated, in the individual and in history. They came to Europe as pious youths, wedded to Buddha, Krishna, Shiva, Vishnu, Kali, Kuanyin, and what not; they touched science, and their ancient faith was shattered as if by a sudden electrical dissolution. Shorn of religious belief, which is the very spirit of India, the Westernized Hindus returned to their country disillusioned and sad; a thousand gods had dropped dead from the skies. They became pessimists and cynics like our own youth in the West today; they had nothing to believe. Inevitably Utopia filled the place of heaven, democracy became a substitute for Nirvana, liberty replaced God. What had gone on in Europe in the second half of the eighteenth century went on now in the East.

Nevertheless the new ideas developed slowly before the War. In 1885 a few Hindu leaders met at Bombay and founded the "Indian National

Congress," but they do not seem at that time to have dreamed even of Home Rule. Those leaders were mostly of the middle and business class; they accepted British rule in India as they accepted the behavior of the sun; they recognized many benefits in that rule; what they wanted was not independence, but a share in the government, its dignities, its powers, and perhaps its spoils. The British office-holders could not understand this point of view; they froze the movement with cold stares and references to the future. Instead, the Viceroy, Lord Curzon, proclaimed, in 1905, his intention to partition Bengal, thereby destroying the unity and strength of the most conscious and powerful community in India. The result was the development of a more rebel mood, and the appearance of blunt leaders like the uncompromising Tilak, who, at the All-India National Congress of 1905, announced to the excited delegates that India must have *Swaraj*. He had created the word[3] out of Sanskrit roots still visible in its English translation, self-rule. Not content with that, the old tiger threatened that if Curzon persisted in the partition of Bengal, India would retaliate with *Swadeshi*, the boycott of foreign goods. In that same eventful year Japan defeated Russia, like another David slaying Goliath; and the East, which for a century had been fearful of the West, took heart, and began to think of all Asia liberating itself from the guns of Europe. It was in 1905, then, that the Indian Revolution began.

II. A Stroke of Politics

In its earlier stages it tended to imitate Russian methods; bombs were exploded, shots were fired, and the "demands" were often in inverse proportion to the strength of the rebels. With the arrival of Gandhi in 1914, and the outbreak of the World War, the situation changed. Gandhi, the idealist, did not realize that the subjection of India was one root of the War; that this had for a century determined British policy, and the size of the British navy, as well as the size of all the navies in the world.[4] Instead, Gandhi saw the War as an opportunity for securing Home Rule by proving the absolute loyalty of India to England. From the beginning to the end of the Great Madness he supported the Allies, and India followed him.

She contributed at once $500,000,000 to the fund for prosecuting the War; she contributed $700,000,000 later in subscriptions to war loans;

and she sent to the Allies various products to the value of $1,250,000,000.[5] The suspension of the Revolutionary movement enabled England to reduce the Indian army to 15,000 men.[6] The total number of Hindus who were persuaded, often by means amounting to compulsion, to fight for England in the war, was 1,338,620, being 178,000 more than all the troops contributed by the combined Dominions of Canada, South Africa, Australia and New Zealand.[7]

None of the Hindu soldiers was granted a commission, however brave he might have proved himself to be.[8] Yet they gave a good account of themselves in France, in Palestine, in Syria and Mesopotamia; a British historian speaks of "the brilliant performances of the Indian contingent sent to France in 1914 at a critical time in the Great War";[9] and some say that it was the Hindu troops who first turned back the Germans at the Marne.[10] Indian soldiers were sent even to China to fight unwillingly against their Asiatic brothers; the Legislature at Delhi questioned the Government about this, but the Government refused to answer.[11] It has been one of the many misfortunes of the Hindus, who are called unfit for self-defense, that they have been considered admirable military material to fight for any others except themselves.

Never had a colony or a possession made so great a sacrifice for the master country. Every Hindu conscious of India looked forward hopefully now, as a reward for this bloody loyalty, to the admission of his country into the fellowship of free dominions under the English flag. Indeed, in 1917, when the position of England in the War was critical, and enthusiasm for the cause of democracy needed stimulation, Mr. Edwin Montagu, Secretary of State for India, made the following announcement in the House of Commons:

> The policy of His Majesty's Government, with which the Government of India are in complete accord, is that of the increasing association of Indians in every branch of the administration and the gradual development of self-governing institutions with a view to the progressive realization of responsible government in India as an integral part of the British Empire. They have decided that substantial steps in this direction should be taken as soon as possible, and that it is of the highest importance as a preliminary to considering what these steps should be that there should be a free and informal exchange of opinion between those in authority at home and in India. His Majesty's Government have accordingly decided, with His Majesty's

> approval, that I should accept the Viceroy's invitation to proceed to India to discuss the matters with the Viceroy and the Government of India, to consider with the Viceroy the views of local Governments, and to receive with him the suggestions of representative bodies and others.
>
> I would add that progress in this policy can only be achieved by successive stages. The British Government and the Government of India, on whom the responsibility lies for the welfare and advancement of the Indian peoples, must be judges of the time and measure of each advance, and they must be guided by the co-operation received from those upon whom new opportunities of service will thus be conferred and by the extent to which it is found that confidence can be reposed in their sense of responsibility.

Shortly thereafter Mr. Montagu visited India, and in collaboration with the Viceroy, Lord Chelmsford, drew up the "Reforms" known by their names. The Secretary wished to carry out his promises liberally, but the Viceroy proved to be an obstinate conservative;[12] these things might do, he said, a generation or two hence. Nor did the Government in London encourage Montagu; the War over, it regretted his promise and sought devices and phrases that would break it while seeming to keep it. Lloyd George, then Premier, declared with unstatesmanlike clarity that Britain intended always to rule India, that there must always remain in India a "steel frame" of British power and British dominance.[13] Some time previously, Lord Curzon had written: "British rule of the Indian people is England's present and future task; it will occupy her energies for as long a span of the future as it is humanly possible to forecast."[14] And Lord Birkenhead was to say, in 1925: "I am not able in any foreseeable future to discern a moment when we may safely, either to ourselves or India, abandon our trust."[15] The last word observed the best traditions of imperialistic hypocrisy.

Therefore the reforms fell far short of what Montagu had hoped for. They established, first, the system of "Dyarchy," by which each province would have two ministries, one responsible to the provincial legislature, and having no powers of any account, the other responsible only to the British authorities, and having all the fundamental powers.[16] Any act of the provincial legislature could be overruled by the Governor, and any act of the Governor, if he considered it necessary to the interests of the Empire, could be passed by decree over the heads of the legislature.[17]

A similar arrangement castrated the Central Assembly; here too the only right was to speak; all authority remained with the Viceroy. He was empowered to enact any measure which might seem necessary to him, even if it must be over a unanimous adverse vote of the Assembly; he could collect taxes which the Assembly had refused to vote; he controlled the expenditures, taxation and defense, and was free to pay salaries and pensions denied by the Assembly. When this remarkable form of progressive self-government reached England, a member of Parliament, Dr. Rutherford, said of it: "Never in the history of the world was such a hoax perpetrated upon a great people as England perpetrated upon India, when in return for India's invaluable service during the War, we gave to the Indian nation such a discreditable, disgraceful, undemocratic, tyrannical constitution."[18]

The Tories[19] have answered that it would have been unwise to give more power to legislatures elected by so illiterate a people—forgetting that one-fifth of the Assembly, and one-half of the upper house, the Council of State, were named by the British Government; that the lower house was elected by a franchise open to one out of two hundred and fifty in the population, and the Council was (half) elected by a franchise still further whittled down. Finally, the voters were divided into sectarian groups—Hindus, Moslems, Christians, Europeans, etc.; they were given representation bearing little relation to their numbers; and each candidate presented himself not to all the citizens in his community, but only to his fellow-sectarians. As Josiah Wedgwood, then a Member of Parliament, said of the Reforms, "The very idea of India vanished from the Bill, to be replaced by the disunited communities of Hindu, Muslim, Sikh, Mahratta, Brahmin, non-Brahmin, Indian Christian, Anglo-Indian, and English."[20] It was claimed that such a plan was necessary to protect the Moslems from the Hindus, who outnumber them almost five to one; in practice, however, it is the Hindus who need protection from the Moslems. The actual result was the increasing division of India into a score of hostile groups.

It was a result admirably suited to an alien ruler, who no doubt had not intended it. It is only a coincidence that Lt.-Col. John Coke, Commandant at Moradadad, advised the British Government, shortly before it took over India from the Company: "Our endeavors should be to uphold in full force the (for us fortunate) separation which exists between the different religions and races, not to endeavor to amalgamate them. *Divide et impera* should be the principle of Indian Government"; to rule your subjects, divide them. It was another coincidence that the British Governor of Bombay, in 1859, sent to his Government this word of counsel: "*Divide et impera* was the old Roman motto, and it should be ours." It was also a coincidence that Sir John Strachey wrote: "The existence, side by side, of hostile creeds among the Indian people is one of the strong points in our political position in India."[21] A government must not be held responsible for the inadvertent honesty of its representatives.

Against the Reforms no Hindu could do anything except protest by tongue or pen. But that was a right not guaranteed to him; the Reforms "did not insure to the Hindus freedom of speech, or of assembly, or of the press; or the right of trial in open court; or the privilege of *habeas corpus*; or any other of the essential rights and privileges which are the foundations and indispensable guarantees of liberty, justice, and law."[22] When protests were tried, and the Hindu press began to voice its suspicion that India had been deceived, the Government at Delhi issued, in 1919, the Rowlatt Acts, re-imposing upon India all those restrictions of assembly, press and speech that had been in effect during the War. The Acts proclaimed that hereafter the Government might arrest without notice or warrant any suspected person, and detain him without trial as long as it liked; that such trial as might be given was to be in secret, before not a jury but three judges appointed by the Government; that the accused need not be told the names of his accusers, nor of the witnesses against him; that these should not be required to confront him; that the accused must not be allowed the right of engaging a lawyer to defend him; that he must not call witnesses in his behalf; that usual legal procedures might be abrogated; and that no appeal would be permitted.[23] An Indian scholar showed that these were almost precisely the rules of the Spanish Inquisition.[24] The Acts were later repealed.

III. A Whiff of Grapeshot

The last blow was the massacre of Amritsar. Since all news of this event remained hidden from the world, and even from Parliament, for several months after its occurrence, and since this slaughter was the proximate cause of the Revolution of 1921, let us inquire into the details. In the now famous city of the Punjab, meetings were held to protest against the Rowlatt Acts; and on March 30th and April 6th, 1919, *hartals* were successfully declared—all business in the city stopping throughout those days as a sign of popular dissatisfaction with the Government. "There was no disorder," says an English clergyman resident in India, "and Europeans passed unmolested among the crowds."[25] It was a fine sample of "non-violent non-co-operation."

On the 9th of April the Government arrested Drs. Kitchlew and Satyapal, who had addressed the protest meetings. When word of this spread, a great crowd poured into the streets; part of it tried to force its way through the police lines to register with the Deputy Commissioner their protest against the arrest of the leaders. Some in the crowd threw stones at the police; the police answered with bullets and ten men were killed. Infuriated by the sight of these dead, the crowd lost all order, destroyed property, and killed five Englishmen. A woman missionary was set upon and beaten, but was carried to safety by some Hindus.

Indians of education tried to pacify the crowd, but failed. Indian officers in the city volunteered their services to the Government.[26]

On the 10th and 11th, 600 troops arrived; on the 12th, Brigadier-General Dyer came, and took command. By that day quiet had been restored, and such crowds as gathered were peaceably dispersed. General Dyer made several arrests; and on the 13th he summoned the people by call of drums, and had read to them a proclamation forbidding them to leave the city without a pass, or to organize processions, or to gather in groups of more than three. Meanwhile 10,000 Hindus from outlying districts, who had little if any knowledge of this proclamation, collected in the enclosure known as Jalianwala Bagh, and proceeded to celebrate a religious festival.[27] The Bagh was an extinct garden, and surrounded with high walls on every side, and entered by a few narrow passages.

Informed of this meeting, General Dyer proceeded to the spot with a detachment of troops equipped with Lewis machine-guns and armored cars. Entering the Bagh, he saw the crowd, and concluded that it had met in violation of his orders. Without giving the slightest warning, or affording the assemblage any opportunity to indicate its pacific intentions, he ordered his troops to fire upon the imprisoned mass; and though the crowd made no resistance, but shouted its horror and despair and pressed in panic against the gates, the General ordered the firing to continue until all the ammunition the soldiers had brought with them was exhausted. He personally directed the firing towards the exits where the crowd was most dense; "the targets," he declared, were "good."[28] The massacre lasted for over ten minutes. When it was over, 1500 Hindus were left on the ground, 400 of them dead.[29] Dyer forbade his soldiers to give any aid to the injured, and by ordering all Hindus off the streets for twenty-four hours, prevented relatives or friends from bringing even a cup of water to the wounded who were piled up in the field.[30]

A reign of official terror followed. General Dyer issued an order that Hindus using the street in which the woman missionary had been beaten should crawl on their bellies; if they tried to rise to all fours, they were struck by the butts of soldiers' guns. He arrested 500 professors and students and compelled all students to present themselves daily for roll-calls, though this required that many of them should walk sixteen miles a day. He had hundreds of citizens, and some school-boys, quite innocent of any crime, flogged in the public square. He built an open cage, unprotected from the sun, for the confinement of arrested persons; other prisoners he bound together with ropes, and kept in open trucks for fifteen hours. He had lime poured upon the naked bodies of *Sadhus* (saints), and then exposed them to the sun's rays that the lime might harden and crack their skin. He cut off the electric and water supplies from Indian houses and ordered all electric fans possessed by Hindus to be surrendered, and given *gratis* to the British. Finally he sent airplanes to drop bombs upon men and women working in the fields.[31]

The news of this barbaric orgy of military sadism was kept from the world for half a year. A belated commission of inquiry appointed by the Government rendered an equivocal report. A committee appointed by the Indian National Congress made a more thorough investigation and reported 1,200 killed, and 3,600 wounded.[32] General Dyer was censured by the House of Commons, exonerated by the House of Lords, and was retired on a pension. Thinking this reward insufficient, the militarists of the Empire raised a fund of $150,-000 for him and presented him with a jeweled sword of honor.[33]

IV. The Revolt of 1921

When he heard of Amritsar, Tagore wrote the following letter to the Viceroy, enclosing the knighthood which had been conferred upon him by the British government.

> The enormity of the measures taken by the Government in the Punjab for quelling some local disturbances has, with a rude shock, revealed to all minds the helplessness of our position as British subjects in India. The disproportionate severity of the punishments inflicted upon the unfortunate people, and the methods of carrying them out, we are convinced, are without parallel in the history of civilized Governments, barring some conspicuous exceptions recent and remote. Considering that such treatment has been meted out to a population disarmed and resourceless by a power which has the most terribly efficient organization for destruction of human lives, we must strongly assert that it can claim no political expediency, far less moral justification. . . .
>
> The accounts of insults and sufferings undergone by our brothers . . . have trickled through the gagged silence, reaching every

> corner of India, and the universal agony of indignation roused in the hearts of our people has been ignored by our rulers—possibly congratulating themselves for imparting what they imagined a salutary lesson.
>
> The time has come when badges of honor make our shame glaring in the incongruous context of humiliation, and I, for my part, wish to stand shorn of all special distinction by the side of my countrymen, who, for their so-called insignificance, are liable to suffer a degradation not fit for human beings.[34]

At the same time Gandhi sent a similar letter to the Viceroy, returning the decorations he had received for services to the Empire in Africa and during the War. On November 4th the National Congress at Delhi, at his suggestion, issued a call for peaceful mass civil disobedience: i.e., for boycott of all British goods, the refusal of all taxes, and the abandonment of all forms of association or co-operation between Hindus and the Government. The British Government thought to mollify resentment by having the Prince of Wales come to India. But when the Prince arrived at Bombay, on November 17th, the city declared a *hartal*, or closing of all business, and left the heir to 320,000,000 Hindus to face empty streets and shut windows. Only the English and a few ambitious Parsee merchants appeared. When the people heard of these latter recalcitrants, they poured out from their hovels and with the characteristically uncontrolled and multiplying rage of the crowd, set fire to the homes of the merchants, and killed fifty-three men.[35]

Gandhi, at Ahmedabad, heard the news with dismay; could it be that his people were as brutal as the British? He rushed to Bombay, and told the crowd, which had greeted him with wild applause, that they had committed an outrage that almost lowered them to the level of General Dyer.

He went back to his *Ashram* a disillusioned man; his people were not prepared for a pacific revolution; like the rest of humanity, they were still too near the beast. He fasted and prayed, and was encouraged to learn that the Prince had found Calcutta a dead city—that there the *hartal* had been carried out with unanimity, and without violence. But at Moplah in the south, and Chauri Chaura, in the north, came two of the blackest events of the first revolt.

The divisions between Moslems and Hindus had suddenly become more violent than before. The revival of Hinduism by Ramakrishna, Vivekananda, and the Arya-Somaj, had widened the gap between the rival sects. Reactionary Hindus played music before mosques, which are not intended to hear music; in some parts of India they classed Moslems with Untouchables; since the Prophet had forbidden the charging of interest, many Mohammedans were in debt to Hindu usurers; the Moslems disapproved of graven images of deity, the Hindus filled the streets with them; the Moslems believed in but one god, and buttoned their coats to the left; the Hindus believed in a thousand gods, and buttoned their coats to the right.[36] From 1923 to 1927 the riots between these two schools of theology cost 450 lives and 5,000 injuries.[37]

The bloodiest of these disagreements occurred at Moplah, on the Malabar coast in the south of India, in August, 1921. The Moplahs were simple Moslems who believed that every murdered Hindu was pleasing in the sight of God. Angered by the British treatment of the Mohammedans in the Near East, they rose against the local officials of the Government, and killed seven of them. Ashamed of their moderation, and finding no other whites to hand, they turned upon the Hindus (to whom they owed money), butchered hundreds of them, and circumcised other hundreds of them, male and female.[38] And at Chauri Chaura, in February, 1922, twenty-seven police who had tried to stop a Nationalist procession were attacked, driven into their barracks, and burned to death.[39] The Government retaliated for these acts of violence by arresting 250,000 men and women.[40]

Gandhi now performed an act of moral courage hardly paralleled in history. He had been empowered by the last National Congress to begin and to end non-co-operation when he should think best. He knew now that many elements in the revolutionary movement secretly rejoiced in the violence at Chauri Chaura and Bombay—the Hindus had proved that they were not cowards: they too could kill. He knew that these younger leaders had no faith in revolution by peace, but were anxious to come to violent grips with the enemy; and he suspected that they looked upon these outbursts of the Hindus as the first events in a successful violent revolution.

But he did not believe that a violent revolution could ever be successful. He had made up his mind that he would rather fail without violence than win with it. He astonished all India, and all England, by issuing instructions to Nationalists everywhere that the non-co-operation movement was to be abandoned at once. A cry of protest came from hundreds of his subordinates; they could not understand. They were convinced that their leader had ruined the Revolution.

And yet that brief revolt had accomplished things hitherto considered impossible. A people overgiven to meditation and prayer, too immersed in other worlds, too ready to accept slavery as Maya—a superficial matter of no importance or reality—had been persuaded, even too suddenly, to turn their thoughts to the earth. A nation which many had looked upon as exhausted and finished had risen like a lusty youth. A people without patriotism and without national consciousness, because divided into a hundred provinces, languages, races, and creeds, had been welded into unprecedented unity. The Hindus stiffened a little, and began to look their masters in the face; the English bent a little, and became more attentive to their serfs. It was evident to all that the Revolution had but begun.

V. Between Revolutions

The influence of Gandhi might have been destroyed by his self-denying ordinance, had not the authorities arrested him soon after its announcement. Now, though his authority had fallen with the leaders, it rose with the people; they hailed him as a martyr and a saint, and put his pictures in their huts along with images of the gods. One poster circulated by his followers showed him as the unchallenged center of a group composed also of Buddha, Krishna, Christ, Tolstoi, Lenin, and McSwiney.[41]

When, in 1924, Gandhi was released, he found his power broken. A new set of leaders had arisen, who called themselves the *Swaraj* Party, and aimed to secure Home Rule through participation in, and legal political capture of, the Government. Those who understood the English smiled at this; but Gandhi was so weakened by failure, fasting, imprisonment and an operation, that he gave a mild consent to the new policy, and retired for years into the obscurity of his *Ashram*.

The new guides of India were of many kinds. There was Chita Ranjan Das, head of the Swarajists; a man of passionate devotion who gave every ounce of his strength to the movement and died of overwork in the prime of life. He thought the *Charka* romantic, and yet feared the possibility that Hindu freedom might be merely a change from foreign to domestic exploiters; he dreaded the development of the factory system in India, and hoped that industry might be spread out through the villages, and its ownership distributed to the point where it would lack the power to dominate the Government.[42] He was an ardent Moderate. "We want to remain within the Empire," he said, "if that is not inconsistent with establishing our own system of government. It is only the lack of vision in the British policy which is driving some of our young men to think of going outside of the Empire."[43]

The older leaders, like Mrs. Annie Besant, an Englishwoman who had lived in India since 1893, became more cautious with every gray hair, and while calling for Home Rule, insisted that the approach to it should be not merely peaceful, but fully in accord with law. Great barristers like Madan Mohan Malaviya, Motilal Nehru, and Vallabhai Patel, who became President of the Assembly at Delhi, exerted their influence to keep the movement within the bounds of law. But the younger Nehru, Jawaharlal, destined to be one of the major leaders in 1930, refused to commit himself to the avoidance of violence; laws made by alien tyrants were not to be respected as laws. A small circle of Communists looked to Russia as a model; a fraction of the industrial workers in the city organized long strikes; and these two groups formed a red fringe on the Nationalist movement. Picturesque as any was Sarojini Naidu, representative of the liberated minority among the women of India; poetess and revolutionary, and fiery orator. See her inflaming with her wild spirit the National Congress which had elected her President:

> Come, my General, come, my soldiers! I am only a woman, only a poet. But as a woman I give to you the weapons of faith and courage, and the shield of fortitude. And as a poet, I fling out the banner of song and sound, the bugle-call to battle. How shall I kindle the flame which shall waken you men from slavery?[44]

VI. The Simon Commission

Into this cauldron of souls came the Simon Commission. The Montagu-Chelmsford Reforms had been tentative; and the British Parliament had arranged to send a commission of inquiry to India, after a decade of the Reforms, to report on their operation, their success or failure, and their possible improvement. The Commission, appointed by a Conservative ministry, consisted of three Conservatives, two Liberals, and two Labor members of Parliament. They sailed for India in January, 1928.

The Hindus had looked forward to this Commission as promising to uncover, for the British people, the defects of the Reforms, and the practical enslavement of India. They were astounded to find that no Hindu had been appointed to its membership. They felt that they could not look for a sympathetic understanding of their situation from men all of them English, most of them conservative, and all of them profiting, indirectly, from the British control of Indian finances and Indian trade. The Hindu leaders, of all groups and sects, announced that so far as they had influence, India would boycott this Commission; they would not lend themselves to the farce of being judged by their enemies.

When the Commission landed at Bombay, on February 3d, 1928, it found the city flying everywhere black flags as a sign of mourning; business was suspended, the shop-windows were shuttered, and the Hindu-owned newspapers had stopped publication for the day. Sir John Simon attempted to undo the mischief by issuing, on his arrival, an invitation to the Indian Assembly to appoint from its membership an "Indian Central Committee" to sit with the Simon Commission on its *second* visit to India. Some Moderates responded, but India paid no attention to them. Wherever the Commission went it was ignored by all those elements in India which desired freedom; and on its appearance great *hartals* were declared in the cities. At the end of March it left India.

It returned in October, 1928, and remained until April, 1929. The boycott still continued. The report of the Commission, to which the liberals of the world had looked for some solution of the problem—how India might be free and yet remain content within the Empire, accepting the compromises necessary to avert a panic in British industry and trade—appeared in 1930, and was received with an amazed disappointment throughout the world. It was made evident, as the "Survey" of surface phenomena was followed by "Recommendations" which were less liberal than the Montagu-Chelmsford Reforms, that the Commission had been unable to rise above a natural resentment at its reception to a sympathetic view of India as, in basic fact, under the heel of England; and that the Conservatives had tried to use the Commission to tighten their grip upon India. It became necessary for the MacDonald Government to exclude all members of the Commission from the Round Table Conference of English and Hindus which had been called for October, 1930. Observers in India agreed that the work of MacDonald and Lord Irwin in pacifying India had been made far more difficult by the Simon Report.

The essence of the Report, so surrounded with historical and argumentative minutiæ that only political experts recognize it as fundamental, is the recommendation that the Central Legislature should be elected no longer by the people, but by the provincial legislatures; that the powers of this "Federal" Assembly should be severely reduced to leave each province almost independent of the central government; and that the power of the provincial governors, and of the Viceroy, should remain as broad as before.

This subtle proposal for the further disunion of India is coated with a suggestion that the franchise for the election of the provincial legislatures shall be extended from the 3% of the population now permitted to vote, to 10%.[45] It suggests that in addition to the property qualification now attached to the franchise, an educational requirement shall be added. (If a certain minimum of education had been made the sole test, it would have been a very fair proposal; however it would have had the disastrous effect of filling the legislatures with men devoted to freedom.) Communal elections are to be continued;[46] it is true that they might be replaced, as in America, by constitutional safeguards against the oppression of religious minorities; but they are now more indispensable than ever to the disunity of India. The system of "Dyarchy" is to be abolished, and the security which it guaranteed to British interests will be protected by the "Over-riding Powers of the Governor." The Governor of each province is not to be elected, of course; he is to be appointed by the British authorities, and he is to remain free to overrule his legislature whenever this seems to him necessary.[47]

The Federal Assembly is to consist of two houses, to each of which the Viceroy will appoint a substantial proportion of its membership. The ratio of Hindus to the British in the Indian Civil Service is not to be raised.[48] The Federal delegates will be responsible not to the people, but to the provincial legislatures. Their membership is to include representatives from the seven hundred Native States,[49] for these, being under native autocrats, do not want Home Rule in India. The Viceroy has the privilege, as before, of overruling the Assembly whenever, in his judgment, the interests of the British Empire are affected.[50] Since India is subject to invasion from without, and sectarian disorders within, like America, its army must remain, "at any rate for a long time to come," under "the control and direction . . . of agents of the Imperial Government."[51] This is obvious; for if the Indian army should be under the control of the country which provides nearly all of its soldiers and all of its funds, the relations between England and India would have to be friendly.

VII. 1930

In December, 1928, the All-India National Congress held a fateful meeting at Calcutta. It had now a dues-paying membership of 510,276, and an attendance of 15,000 men and women from every section of India. Shortly before, the Viceroy, Lord Irwin, had sought to appease discontent by promising India Home Rule in the future;

but as this was no more than Mr. Montagu had promised eleven years back, the Hindu leaders returned his note as being worthless without a date. Sick of these vague references to the future —promises apparently made in the hope that "things would blow over"—the Congress of Calcutta served notice that unless dominion status were granted to India by the end of 1929, placing her on an equality with Canada, South Africa, Australia and New Zealand, the members of the Congress pledged themselves to inaugurate, on January 1, 1930, a movement for complete independence. If India could not be treated like Canada it would seek freedom like the United States. Gandhi pled with the Congress to make the interval two years instead of one; it refused; and he accepted its decision.

On New Year's Day of 1930 the National Congress met at Lahore. It observed that the Government had made no advance toward the liberation of India, except to announce, on November 1, 1929, that Great Britain proposed to call a Round Table Conference to discuss a new constitution for India. Asked if the new constitution would give dominion status, Lord Irwin had replied that it was the intention of His Majesty's Government to give India dominion status "ultimately." The Congress expressed its understanding of this word by empowering Gandhi and an Executive Committee to declare, at their discretion, the opening of the campaign for freedom. After an interval of modest retirement, Gandhi had been accepted once more as the leader of India.

On March 6th, he called the Indian people to another trial of *Satyagraha* and *Ahimsa*—civil disobedience without violence; and he wrote to the Viceroy explaining his action.

> Before embarking on civil disobedience, ... I would fain approach you and find a way out. I cannot intentionally hurt anything that lives, much less fellow human beings. . . . While therefore I hold British rule a curse, I do not intend to harm a single Englishman or any legitimate interest he may have in India. . . . I do not consider Englishmen in general to be worse than any other people on earth. I have the privilege of claiming many Englishmen as my dearest friends. . . . Why do I regard British rule as a curse? It has impoverished the dumb millions by a system of progressive exploitation and by the ruinously expensive military and civil administration which the country cannot afford. It has reduced us politically to serfdom.

The Viceroy replied very briefly:

> His Excellency . . . regrets to learn that you contemplate a course of action which is clearly bound to involve violation of the law and danger to the public peace.

On March 12th Gandhi began his "march to the sea." He stopped at villages on the way and instructed the people not to pay the salt tax, which weighed so heavily upon the millions. On April 16th he reached the coast, and made salt by evaporating ocean water, thus violating a Government monopoly. On the 9th two of his sons were arrested. On the 14th, the younger Nehru, President of the National Congress, was arrested for manufacturing salt, and Sen Gupta, Mayor of Calcutta, was imprisoned for sedition. On May 3d Gandhi was for the second time sent to jail.

Meanwhile the people were showing heroism hardly precedented in history. At Peshawar, on April 23d, a crowd gathered in protest against the arrest of local Nationalist leaders. The official reports of what followed stated that twenty people were killed in a riot. The report of Abdul Kasuri, President of the Punjab Provincial Congress Committee, was smuggled through the censorship. As its simple story proceeds, these distant things cease to be phrases, and become realities of flesh and flowing blood.

> There had been absolutely no disorder, and not the least cause given to the authorities to fear that there would be any. . . . The crowd had been behaving throughout in an exemplary manner. . . .
>
> While the crowd was returning towards the city, two armored cars full of soldiers came from behind without blowing the horn or giving any notice whatever of their approach, and drove into the crowd regardless of consequences. Many people were brutally run over, several were wounded, and at least three died on the spot. In spite of the provocation, the crowd still behaved with great restraint. . . .
>
> At this time an English officer on a motorcycle came dashing past. As to what happened to him it is not quite clear. There are two conflicting versions. The semi-Government version says that he fired into the crowd, and one of the persons who was wounded by the shot struck him on the head and he died. The other version . . . is that he collided with the motor car. . . .
>
> At the same time one of the armored cars caught fire. . . . It is alleged on the one hand that it was set fire to by the mob; the other version is that it caught fire accidentally. . . . A troop of English soldiers had reached the spot, and without any warning, began firing into the crowd, in which there were women and children. . . .

Now the crowd gave a good example of the lesson of non-violence that had been instilled into them. When those in front fell down wounded, . . . those behind came forward with their breasts bared and exposed themselves to the fire. . . . Some people got as many as twenty-one bullet wounds in their bodies. . . . All the young people stood their ground without getting into a panic. A young Sikh boy came and stood in front of a soldier and asked him to fire at him, which the soldier unhesitatingly did, killing him. Similarly, an old woman, seeing her relations and friends being wounded, came forward, was shot, and fell down wounded. An old man with a four-year old child on his shoulders advanced, asking the soldier to fire at him. He was taken at his word and he also fell down wounded. Scores of such instances will come out on further inquiry.

The crowd kept standing at the spot . . . and were fired at from time to time until there were heaps of dead and dying lying about. The Anglo-Indian paper of Lahore, which represents the official view, wrote to the effect that the people came forward one after another to face the firing, and when they fell wounded they were dragged back and others came forward. This state of things continued from 11 o'clock to 5 P.M. . . .

Two facts are noteworthy. . . . There was not one single instance where there was the mark of a bullet at the back. . . . Neither the police nor the military nor anybody else alleges that there was any stick or weapon,

> blunt or sharp, with the persons in the crowd, nor were any wrenched from any person by the authorities.
>
> At this stage it is very difficult to say what is the number of the dead and wounded. This much seems most likely, that the number of the dead is in hundreds, and a careful study of the situation seems to disclose this incident to be a repetition of the Jalianwala Bagh massacre.[52]

At Dharasana the *Satyagrahi*, or revolutionists pledged to peace, expressed the feeling of India that a vital necessity like salt should not be taxed, by attempting to walk up to the salt pans and carry away what they needed. It was a little illogical, for they do not seem to have offered any payment. The police, stolid Hindus from Surat under British officers, did their best to repel the advance without violence; they held great bamboo sticks or *lathis*, six feet long with *steel* knobs on the ends, over the heads of the vanguard, and threatened them. When the advance persisted, the police struck. The revolutionists made no resistance, but continued to approach the police until their front ranks fell unconscious from repeated blows. A corps of stretcher-bearers had come prepared, and while these carried away the fallen, the second rank advanced to the police, without raising an arm or carrying any weapon. They too were struck on the head, in the abdomen, and in the face, until they fell. This continued for hours, till hundreds lay unconscious and bleeding on the ground, on stretchers, or in neighboring homes. Mr. Webb Miller, European News Manager of the United Press, an eyewitness, writes:

> In eighteen years of reporting in twenty-two countries, during which I have witnessed innumerable civil disturbances, riots, street-fights and rebellions, I have never witnessed such harrowing scenes as at Dharasana. The Western mind can grasp violence returned by violence, can understand a fight, but is, I found, perplexed and baffled by the sight of men advancing coldly and deliberately and submitting to beating without attempting defense. Sometimes the scenes were so painful that I had to turn away momentarily.
>
> One surprising feature was the discipline of the volunteers. It seemed they were thoroughly imbued with Gandhi's non-violence creed.[58]

At Bombay, on June 19th and 21st, this strange capacity to suffer without striking back, as a mute sign of India's new pride and resolution, was demonstrated again. Orderly battalions of *Satyagrahi*, men and women, marched up in succession to Maidan Esplanade to hold a meeting forbidden by the government, and allowed themselves to be beaten down unconscious by the Mahratti police. Powerful Sikhs, armed with great swords, joined with these *Satyagrahis*, and, refusing to defend themselves, allowed their heads to be beaten until they fell to the ground with blood streaming from their mouths.[54] No one in India had thought that this war-like race would accept the counsels of Gandhi. These were scenes unknown in history since the Coliseum; it was as if the primitive Christians were once again fighting with silent suffering against an oppressive Rome.

Throughout these pitiful massacres one could still sympathize with the police. They had been told to prevent a violation of the "law"; they could not be expected to distinguish between law made by the representatives of India, and law imposed upon 320,000,000 Hindus by a few invading foreigners; they only knew how to obey. "They seemed reluctant to strike. It was noticeable that when the officers were occupied on other parts of the line the police slackened, only to resume threatening and beating when the officers appeared again."[55] But in many cases the brutality without which no man would be allowed to be a policeman in India appeared in the most repulsive forms.

One eyewitness reports: "The police snatch off the men's garments, twist and squeeze the testicles, and even batter them until their victims foam at the mouth and become unconscious."[56] This incredible story is corroborated by another witness apparently above suspicion. On June 12th Miss Madeline Slade, an Englishwoman of high standing, daughter of an Admiral in the British Navy, printed in Gandhi's weekly, *Young India*, the following account of what she had seen at Dharasana—items either not included in the United Press report or expunged from it by the censor:

> During these days when the authorities in Whitehall and Simla are never tired of extolling the behavior of the police, I thought I would go and see for myself how this "exemplary behavior" has affected the *Satyagrahis* at Dharasana. I reached Bulsar at mid-day on June 6th, just as the wounded were being brought in there from the "raid" of that morning. Many of them were being carried on stretchers, others could just struggle from the motors to hospital wards.
>
> "The beating and torturing has been most merciless today!" said the doctors and attendants. I proceeded around the rooms to visit the *Satyagrahis* more closely and to take notes from doctors as to the nature of their wounds. Literally I felt my skin to creep and my hair to stand on end as I saw those brave

men, who but a few hours previously had gone forth absolutely unarmed, vowed to non-violence, now lying here before me battered and broken from head to foot. Here was a young man with his shoulders and buttocks so beaten that he could not lie on his back, yet his arms and sides were so damaged that he did not know how to turn for rest. There was another gasping for breath with his chest badly battered, and nearby was a strong, tall Musselman lying utterly helpless.

"What are his damages?" I asked.

"He has received fearful blows on the stomach, the back and right leg," they replied. "Also his testicles are both swollen, having been badly squeezed by the police."

We went upstairs. Here my attention was attracted by the sounds of sharp-drawn, whistling breathing, intermixed with heart-rending groans. It was a young man writhing in agony. He kept catching at his stomach, and at intervals he would suddenly sit up as if he were going to go mad with pain.

"He has had a deadly blow right on the abdomen," they said. "And he has been vomiting blood. He has also had his testicles severely squeezed, which has shattered his nerves."

They fetched ice and applied it to the head and damaged parts, which gradually soothed him.

And so we went on from this house to another, where we found still more and more wounded. Everyone to whom I talked gave the same description of fiendish beating, torturing, thrusting and dragging, and one and all spoke with burning horror of the foul abuse and unspeakable blasphemy which the police and their Indian and English superiors had poured upon them.

So this is some of the exemplary behavior of the police. . . . What then has become of English honor, English justice? . . . Who could dare to uphold as a means of dispersing a non-violent gathering: 1. *Lathi* blows on head, chest, stomach and joints; 2. Thrusts with *lathis* in private parts, abdominal regions; 3. Stripping of men naked before beating; 4. Tearing off loin cloths and thrusting of sticks into anus; 5. Pressing and squeezing of the testicles until a man becomes unconscious; 6. Dragging of wounded men by legs and arms, often beating them the while; 7. Throwing of wounded men into thorn hedges or salt water; 8. Riding of horses over men as they lie or sit on the ground; 9. Thrusting of pins and thorns into men's bodies, sometimes even when they are unconscious; 10. Beating of men after they had become unconscious, and other vile things too many to relate. . . .

The whole affair is one of the most devilish, cold-blooded and unjustifiable in the history of nations. India has now realized the true nature of the British *Raj* (rule), and with the realization the *Raj* is doomed.[57]

The Government did not protest that this description was untrue. It merely ordered *Young India* to deposit $18,000 as a guarantee against the publication of such articles in the future. The magazine refused, because it could not. The Government suppressed it, and confiscated its property.

That is all we are told, for over the great sacrifice the censor has drawn the veil, lest we should be too much moved. Behind the censor and the veil God knows what is happening in India, what courage and suffering, what shooting and bombing, what airplanes and tanks, what self-control of the spirit, unknown in history, before power and terror and guns.

Meanwhile, as the printer prints these words, the Round Table Conference opens in London. All the parties of England are represented there by able men; but from India have come only unrepresentative delegates, scorned by the nation. Gandhi, Nehru *père et fils,* Malaviya, Patel, Sarojini Naidu and a hundred other leaders chosen by India to speak for it, are in jail.

What will the British do? They have the power—all the weapons of land and sea and air, an iron control of the Hindu press, and a propaganda organization in every part of the world, subtle and influential beyond belief. They do not yet need to be just. Perhaps they will suggest to Parliament only enough liberty for India as will leave it still at the mercy of England, but will split the Nationalists into those willing, and those unwilling, to welcome a crumb. So the British may disrupt the present movement, turn the leaders upon one another, and then, when the movement has broken up, rest on their arms until they must fight again.

But then they *will* have to fight again. A people so aroused, so patient and so tenacious, will not forget. The play is not over. 1921 was the First Act; 1930 was the Second Act. There will be a Third.

CHAPTER FOUR

THE CASE FOR ENGLAND

I described in Chapter I the appalling condition of India today. That description was colored with the prejudices natural to an American; it stated the case for India without pretense of offering the other side. I wish now to present the English point of view as completely as I can in narrow compass; to let England speak for herself, through her own capable defenders; and to reserve all rejoinder until this defense is complete.[1]

I. England Speaks

1. The Nietzschean Defense

Ultimately the case for England's hold on India rests upon the Nietzschean ethic of power—on the right of the stronger to use the weaker for his purposes. Sir William Joynson-Hicks, Home Minister in the Baldwin Government, expressed the matter candidly some years ago. "I know it is said in missionary meetings that we conquered India to raise the level of the Indians. That is cant. We conquered India as an outlet for the goods of Great Britain. We conquered India by the sword, and by the sword we shall hold it."[2]

For the Hindus (henceforth it is the British who speak) are a lower race, doomed by their climate to some foreign yoke. The heat of the sun and the aridity of the soil have made India inevitably weak, and therefore poor, and therefore ignorant; it is so incapable of self-preservation and self-government that its entire known history is the story of its repeated invasion by successful conquerors. Four thousand years ago the Aryans came down out of the north, and created a state and a civilization; the heat destroyed their vitality, and they decayed. Seven hundred years ago the Mohammedans came down out of the north, and created a state and a civilization; the heat destroyed their vitality, and they decayed. Four hundred years ago the Mongols came down out of the north, and created a state and a civilization; the heat destroyed their vitality, and they decayed. When the Mogul Empire in India broke up at the opening of the eighteenth century, India naturally fell a prey to new invaders, new rulers unweakened by her heat. If England had not taken her, France would have done it, or Portugal, or Holland; it was her good fortune to be conquered by the greatest organizers and fairest rulers of the modern world.

The earlier conquerors remained in India, and lost their strength; the British come afresh in each generation from the north, and their officials in India return every fifth year to renew their vigor amid England's snows and rains; this is why 68,000 Englishmen can rule 320,000,000 Hindus. Look at a British officer in India, and then look at a Hindu—peasant or proletaire, poet or philosopher; you will understand at a glance how inevitable and natural is the mastery of the one and the submission of the other.

It is childish romanticism to idealize the Hindu; young intellectuals enjoy a sense of superiority in patronizing the weak. But Katherine Mayo has exposed this idealization once for all. Read her scornful pages and see the Hindus as they are: a people defeated by caste and introverted by slavery; sunk in such superstition as no other nation on earth would bear with; millions of them in every year coming from great distances to bathe in filthy rivers as a magic means of securing a wealthy reincarnation, or, if they are lucky, eternal apathy and everlasting death; millions of them offering animal sacrifices to Kali, the goddess with blood-dripping jaws; thirty millions of them starving while seventy million "sacred" cows roam the streets leisurely, never slaughtered for Hindu food; a million "holy men" sitting in naked idleness on bathing ghats, or swings, or beds of nails, consuming without producing; 164,000,000 women enslaved to men, some of them digging ditches, others carrying burdens six hours a day for ten cents a day, some of them ministering as temple prostitutes to acquisitive and lecherous priests, half of them shut in by *purdah* in close and stuffy *zenanas*, doomed to ignorance and disease; two million girls married, and one million of them widowed, by the age of ten; 26,000,000 widows forbidden to seek a second mate; temples adorned with phallic statuary showing gods and goddesses in various forms of sexual intercourse; men divided inevitably by birth into two thousand castes, Brahmins scorning Sudras, Sudras scorning Pariahs; 44,500,000 Pariahs or "Untouchables" excluded by the caste system from most of the schools, from the use of public wells, from any contact or association with their betters, who deliberately keep them in ignorance and slavery; these Outcastes living in squalor unequaled elsewhere in the world—their miserable alleys serving as cesspools, sewers and privies—while rich Brahmins and native potentates hoard gold, flash jewelry, and live in idle luxury; a nation poorer than any, and yet multiplying beyond measure and beyond control under the protection of British sanitation and British guns: these are the people who lecture the English on morality, and pretend that they are fit for democracy; these are the superstitions and abuses behind that poverty and illiteracy which the simple-minded attribute to foreign rule.[3]

2. British Contributions to India

No; it is clear that a people so weakened and stupefied needs for a long time to come the guidance of a race that will bring them hygiene and hospitals, schools and colleges, science and technology, officers and administrators, and a careful preparation for self-rule under the tutelage of the freest and best-governed of modern states. That this external management of India has been a boon to her, one fact alone suffices to prove, and that is the enormous growth of India's population under the British régime. Irrigation works directed by British engineers have added 20,000,000 acres to the cultivable land[4]—an area equal to France. The Sukkur Barrage, now nearing completion, will bring under irrigation a region as large as cultivated Egypt.[5] Already 13% of the tilled acreage of India is supplied by Government irrigation.[6] If the Hindu peasant remains poor despite these great improvements, and despite the labors of the Government to spread agricultural education, it is because he is superstitiously attached to ancestral methods and implements; because he indebts himself to usurious money-lenders, all of his own race, to pay for extravagant dowries and costly festivals; and because his Nationalist leaders have not had the intelligence to see, or the courage to say, that the root of Indian poverty lies in ignorant and reckless breeding. What India needs is not a Gandhi, nor even a Tagore, but a Malthus to teach it the laws of population, and a Voltaire to free it from superstition by laughing to death its ridiculous gods.

No romantic return to medieval simplicity with Gandhi's spinning-wheel will solve the problem of India's poverty; it can be solved only by science and industry. Granted that the factories of India, most of them owned now by Hindu capitalists, exploit their workers after the fashion of all nascent industrial systems; these are the measles and whooping-cough of industry, and will be cured. Granted that the factory-workers are underpaid; but they work far more leisurely, and with far less skill, than the workingmen of Europe or America; and at sowing or harvest time they are as likely as not to abandon their factories and return to their villages, making orderly and economical production impossible.[7] Meanwhile Factory Acts have been passed, shortening the hours and improving the conditions of labor; machinery and skilled workers, technicians and capital, have been brought in to transform India into an efficient nation. The construction of telegraph, telephone and postal systems, of electric light and power plants, and 40,000 miles of railways, has opened the path for the growth of India to wealth and pride. Already the life and mind of the country have been quickened by these unwelcomed innovations from the West; the new speed of communication and travel has jarred the Hindus from their dogmatic slumber, and prepared them to compete with the peoples of the modern world.

If India has seen the decay of her old domestic handicrafts, it is because she rejected modern machinery and methods, and thought she could stand still and yet remain wealthy, while half the earth was moving forward into industry. The Abbé Dubois predicted a century ago that the scorn of the Brahmins for Western ideas and tools would leave India becalmed and impoverished in the wake of a progressive Europe.[8] If she has for a hundred years exported more goods than she has received, it is because since the days of Pliny she has preferred to import gold rather than goods, and chosen to hoard her riches, or to congeal them into jewelry, rather than invest them in productive enterprise. Even Gandhi has admitted that this withholding of gold and silver from circulation is a main source of India's poverty;[9] and Sir Valentine Chirol has calculated that if the wealth thus hoarded during the last half-century had been liberated to finance and stimulate industry, the proceeds would now suffice to discharge the whole of India's public debt.[10]

To make up for this spinster timidity of the Hindus, the English have established 70,000 co-operative credit societies to displace the ruthless money-lender, and have lent vast sums to India at rates of interest far lower than those demanded by Indian investors. The Indian railways were built, and the factories of India were equipped, with British capital; $2,500,000,000 have been invested by Europeans in Hindu industries; and most of the $3,500,000,000 national debt represents loans from England.[11] The "drain" from India to England today is mostly composed of moderate interest charges on these British loans.

India has never sent a penny of tribute to England; she has merely paid for services received, for financial, technical, administrative and medical aid. If India no longer exercises economic mastery over nations that once acknowledged its sway, this has been due not to political injustice, but to the normal processes of economic change. All life is war, and the victories of industry and trade may be as decisive as those on the battlefield. Economic competition among nations is as legitimate as among individuals; that India has lost, and England won, is an historical accident, not a British crime. For many centuries, in the war between East and West, Asia held the rôle of aggressor against Europe. That mastery was lost when trade abandoned land routes for the sea; and nations that relied on handicrafts were doomed by the Industrial Revolution. Until India learns modern ways of production, it will naturally and inevitably be subject to some modern state.

But even to speak of "India" is to confess the beneficence of English rule. For until England came to her, India did not exist; there was no political entity called India, but only a congeries of independent states, forever at war. Even today there is no Hindu word for all Indians, no language common to them; their revolutionaries themselves use and propose English as the only possible speech to unite all Hindus across the barriers of their two hundred dialects.[12] Even today there are in India seven hundred "Native States," ruled by native princes subject to England only in foreign affairs; these princes strongly object to the severance of India from the British Empire, and would refuse, if necessary at the cost of civil war, to submit to an Indian parliament. It is British discipline and order that have kept the peace for a century among these many states, these hostile religions and divisive castes; it is British soldiers who are asked for by every community to preserve the peace between Hindus and Mohammedans. It is a British-trained army, and a British-paid navy, that have protected India for a hundred years from invasion by land or sea, from wild tribes on the north and from land-hungry empires like Japan. It is a British judiciary that has given to India an enlightened code of civil and criminal law, administered impartially to all; it is Western missionary enterprise that has rescued the Outcaste from Brahmin scorn, given him medicine and education, and infused into him some saving hope and pride.

And it is from England that India has taken that ideal of democracy which now agitates its revolutionaries. India has never been democratic, either in practice or in theory; has never offered its people equal opportunity in economic, political, or social life. But under British rule the Hindus have developed legislatures and ministries with extensive powers; provincial services are almost entirely manned by natives; and the admission of the Hindus to self-government despite their dangerous factionalism and illiteracy has gone on at a pace which has alarmed many careful observers.

For it is clear that India is not yet ripe for full democracy; only a young intellectual who has no thought of facing the realities and responsibilities of administration could imagine a stable and competent government issuing from the universal adult suffrage of these 320,000,000 heads, so full of superstition and fanaticism. The sudden transportation of modes of government from advanced nations to backward nations is no longer advocated by any mature mind; and the only reason why all responsible elements in India do not denounce this scheme is that some of them hope to profit by its miscarriage. "The success of Gandhi," says a Hindu, Sankara Nair, "would be the success of the forces of reaction in their attempt to attain what they call national independence, which in reality means their sole dominion."[13] There are a thousand Hindu capitalists waiting to exploit India unhindered when it is "free."

We cannot speak of English contributions to the improvement of Hindu religious life, for the passionate conservatism of India closes this field to all external reform. But one by one most of the moral abuses have yielded to British patience and suggestion, from the abolition of suttee in 1829 to the practical ending of child marriage in 1929. We must attribute to foreign influence and example the rising status of women in India, the increasing remarriage of widows, the introduction of birth control, and the improvement in the condition of the Untouchables.

If these moral reforms make but a modest sum, the cultural contributions of England to India are beyond exaggeration. It was European scholars, chiefly English, who studied the languages and cultures of ancient India, and resurrected Vedic literature and wisdom; it was Europe that revealed India to the Hindus.[14] Before Sir William Jones and Max Müller, history had been to the Hindus mere Maya—surface appearance and delusion, deserving only to be ignored; now it set the Indian imagination afire, and Hindu Nationalists, like the Romantics of Schlegel's day, turned to warm their faith in their country at the hearth of her idealized past. India became interested in learning, in scholarship, at last even in science; schools financed by the Government and by the foreign missions won over the distrustful students, and Western education, which a Hindu historian calls "the greatest of blessings India has gained under British rule,"[15] began its attack upon superstition, ignorance and sloth. India, mentally stagnant for almost a thousand years, had waited for just such alien seed to fertilize it; in the crossing of these cultures, Oriental and Western—in the stinging contact of East and West, of religion and science, of handicrafts and industry—lay the source of that Indian Renaissance which has begotten so prematurely the Indian Revolution.[16] The East is drunk with the wine of the West, with the lust for liberty, luxury and power.

3. The Key to the White Man's Power

But liberty is impossible in the modern world, if only because nations are too interdependent economically to be ever again quite free, until our industrial civilization ends. Wherever industry replaced agriculture it compelled the importation of food and—to pay for the food—the exportation of manufactured goods; it compelled the search for raw materials and markets; it compelled peoples dependent in this way upon foreign areas to protect their own security by acquiring control of those areas; it compelled imperialism. There is a manifest destiny, but it is economic rather than political; and one of its laws is that any people unable to develop the resources of its soil for the needs of the world is fated to be ruled, directly or indirectly, by a people capable of promoting the development of that soil. Englishmen driven from farms to factories by the Industrial Revolution would have starved to death in their great cities if they had not been able to find foreign raw materials, fuel and food. They found them, and made them secure for England; it is what any nation would have done, what all nations do. That is the essence of modern history.

So, by the impersonal process of economic evolution, England has become dependent upon India; and any sudden severance of their relations would be politically dangerous for India, and economically ruinous for England. Consider what would happen if India were at once to receive complete Home Rule: she would pass legislation involving the loss of a billion dollars to European investors; she would put up a high tariff on British goods, and throw a million British workingmen into the swollen ranks of the unemployed; she would teach all her growing generation a hatred of Western civilization; she would dismiss British civil servants and British officers, destroy the efficiency of the Indian army, open the frontier to Afghan tribes and Russian encroachments, and put an end to the British Empire.

For a century Russia has been advancing into Southern Asia; now she controls the new Soviet republics of Turkmanistan, Uzbekia, Taikistan, and Kara Khirgis. Let England step out of India, and Russia will step in. India and China will join Russia in a Soviet federation that will wage a bitter economic battle, and perhaps mobilize a billion Asiatics, in a war of the continents to destroy European trade and Western civilization. The greatest system of order ever built—the British Commonwealth—is at stake; the security of travel, the safety of white men in Asiatic states, the peace and existence of Australia and New Zealand, the whole prestige and leadership of the white race on the globe, are imperiled by the Indian Revolution. Give India Home Rule, and she will demand equality with Canada, South Africa and Australia; give her this equality, and she will demand freedom of Hindu emigration to these countries; permit this, and the standard of living all over the world will sink to the Asiatic level. A German professor, George Wegener, expressed the heart of the matter as far back as 1911: "It is in India, of all places on the earth, that the superiority of the white over the colored races is most strikingly demonstrated. If the Asiatics were to succeed in destroying English mastery there, then the position of the whole white race throughout the world would be fatally undermined."[17]

It is not a choice between theories that confronts us, it is a choice between Asia and ourselves; between life as it is lived by Pariahs and coolies, and life as it has been enriched in Europe and America by industry and trade. When England is compelled to leave India it will mark the inauguration of Asia's mastery of the globe.

II. India Answers

This is the case for refusing Home Rule to India. What has the Hindu to say to it?

1. Morals in India

He will remind the English how indignantly they denounced, in 1914, the Nietzschean ethic which in the last resort is the only ground on which the British retention of India can be defended today. He will attribute the subjugation of 320,000,000 Hindus by 68,000 Englishmen not to the climate of India,[18] but to the historical accident that England found India helpless in 1757, disarmed her, and, by control of the seas, has kept her weaponless ever since. He will protest against comparing the conduct, superstitions, and intellect of a people oppressed and kept ignorant for a century with those of nations reaping now the harvest of a century of liberty and public education. He will wonder whether British refusal to "interfere" with Hindu religion was not due in some measure to a sense of the great advantage, to an alien government, of a creed that stupefied men with myth and ritual, and consoled them for earthly suffering with dreams of future bliss. He will recall to the West its own superstitions, recently gathered together by Professor Richet in his book on *Idiot Man,* and he will suggest that Hindu superstitions are not worse than ours, but merely different; he will compare Lourdes with Benares, and remark on the popularity, among us, of new religions that reject medicine and seek to heal with faith. He will picture vast crowds flocking to a grave in quest of miraculous cures; he will point out that the central item in our religious ritual is a relic of savage theophagy. He will admire our sympathy for the goats sacrificed to Kali, and will offer his own to the thousands of cattle slaughtered at Chicago every day. He will acknowledge the evils of the caste system, and inquire whether the attitude of a Brahmin to a Pariah differs, except in words, from that of a British lord to a navvy, or a Park Avenue banker to an East Side huckster, or a white man to a negro, or a European to an Asiatic.

He will regret the early age of marriage in India,[19] and its unnatural deferment here; he will mourn over child widows in India, and child laborers in America—a million and a half children under thirteen in the factories of the United States.[20] He will compare the hostility of Moslems and Hindus in India to the recent riots of Protestants against Catholics in Liverpool, the Know-nothing outbreaks of the last century in America, the genial persuasiveness of the Ku Klux Klan, and the part played by religion in the presidential election of 1928. He will voice his sorrow for the wars of the Hindu princes, and the War of the Nations; for the subjection of women in India, and the subjection of men in America; for the disabilities of the Untouchables there, and the lynching of negroes here. He will admit that adultery is not as highly developed in India as in more prosperous countries. He will comment gently on the popularity of murder and fornication in the United States; on our superiority in criminal gangs and political machines; on the break-down of government in our cities, and the unsafety of life in our streets and our homes; on our riots of drunkenness in America and in Paris; on the spread of sexual promiscuity and disease, and the disappearance of professional prostitution; on the erotomania of our colleges, our night-life, our stage, and our literature; on the primitive vulgarity of our motion-pictures and our musical comedies; on the decay of marriage and the home, and the passage of order and discipline from our lives.

No doubt every civilization has its faults, and only the most unfair mind would present a list of the faults as a description of the civilization. An American may still love America despite the evils which he finds within its borders; he may still object to foreign control of American cities despite their evident unfitness for self-government. The Hindu has been the first to acknowledge the abuses of his country. From over a century ago, when Ram Mohan Roy initiated the movement to abolish suttee, down to 1929, when the Hindu legislature, against the original opposition of the British Government in India,[21] raised the age of marriage to fourteen for women and eighteen for men, it is native reform organizations like the Brahmo-Somaj and the Arya-Somaj that have fought the best fight against child-marriage, perpetual widowhood, caste, bloody sacrifices, polytheism, and idolatry. "The roll-call of those associated in the movement to secure more humane treatment for the Outcastes is long and illustrious."[22] Gandhi has risked his whole position on the liberation of the Untouchables; he has adopted an Outcaste girl as his own, and refuses to enter any home whose doors are closed to her.

"I loathe and detest child-marriage," says Gandhi; "I shudder to see a child-widow. I have never known a grosser superstition than that the Indian climate causes sexual precocity. What does bring about untimely puberty is the mental and moral atmosphere surrounding family life."[23] Nothing could be more straightforward; indeed there are many who believe that Gandhi is here too hard on his people. "We must compare a girl of fifteen in India with one of seventeen in England," says Ernest Wood.[24] "Personally," said Lajpat Rai, "I consider it a social crime to marry a girl under the age of sixteen, even though Indian girls reach puberty about the age of twelve."[25] "It can be safely said that a young girl of twelve in India is as old as a young woman of fifteen in America."[26] Those who like to be generous would add that large classes of Hindu society avoid child-marriage;[27] that, according to the official census of India,[28] child-marriage is merely betrothal, the girl remaining with her parents until puberty, and only then consummating the union; that 60% of the girls marry after fifteen;[29] that consummation before the age of thirteen has long been illegal;[30] that the average age of first motherhood in India is 18.3 years.[31] Finally, we must do what justice we can to the purpose behind the institution of child-marriage—the acceptance of it as preferable both to premarital promiscuity and to the choice of mates under the blinding influence of erotic desire.[32] Sexual irregularities are much rarer in India than in almost any other country. We may entertain every expectation, however, that India will soon emulate America, and replace early marriage with promiscuity.

In no other country is the reformation of moral abuses progressing so rapidly as in India. Child-marriage is already ended, and "the vast majority of Hindus remarry their widows"; compulsory widowhood will probably disappear in a generation. In 1915 fifteen widows married; in 1925,

2,663.[33] The temple dancers, or Devadasis, are almost extinct; every tourist searches for them and finds none. The seclusion of women is breaking down; the Revolutionary movement has brought them into the open with almost Western precipitation. A number of periodicals for women discuss the most up-to-date problems; even a birth-control league has appeared.[34] The cities are breaking down *purdah* day by day, until now hardly 6% of the women observe it;[35] modest women walk the streets unveiled and unabashed. In many of the provinces women vote and hold political office; twice women have been president of the Indian National Congress. Many of them have taken degrees at the universities, and have become doctors, lawyers, and professors.[36] Soon, no doubt, the tables will be turned, and women will rule. Must not some wild Western influence bear the guilt of this appeal issued by a subaltern of Gandhi to the women of India?

> "Away with ancient *purdah*! Come out of the kitchens quick! Fling the pots and pans rattling into corners! Tear the cloth from your eyes, and see the new world! Let your husbands and brothers cook for themselves. There is much work to be done to make India a nation!"[37]

Such is the result of the "fertilization of the Orient with Western ideas." We cannot tell yet whether this intellectual seduction of a sub-continent will prove to be a favor or a curse.

2. The Decay of Caste

The greatest evil of all remains. Caste was once a necessity, a cordon of marriage restrictions flung between conquerors and conquered to keep the Aryan blood pure and the stock strong; even to-day we would not ask the high-caste Brahmin to lie down with the unwashed and omnivorous Pariah. There is in caste a hygienic and eugenic element in accord with the most modern biological ideas. And all through Indian history the castes were rather occupational guilds than ethnic strata or political cliques; every trade constituted a caste; and if the Brahmins formed a caste it was largely because they were united by their functions as teachers and priests.

It is only with the passing of the handicrafts, and the coming of urban industry, that the caste system has become an anachronism. Heredity of trades, so reasonable in domestic industry, is an impediment in cities and factories. The Industrial Revolution dissolved all class-formations, and generated democracy, by demanding and using talent from every corner and every rank. It is on the program of our century, no doubt, to destroy the caste system in India, not by agitation, but by impersonal economic evolution. Already the factories are mingling Brahmins, Vaisyas, Kshatryas, Sudras and Untouchables; the mines are mingling them; the trams and trains are mingling them; the co-operatives and the schools are mingling them; one writer believes, too optimistically, that caste will, in effect, be destroyed within twenty years.[38] The Kshatryas and Vaisyas have practically disappeared. The lower castes have elected mayors in large cities; the ruler of Baroda, the most advanced of Indian states, is a Sudra; the Maharajah of Gwalior is a Sudra; the Maharajah of Mysore is a Vaisya; the Maharajah of Kashmir receives all castes and creeds indifferently at his court; women of every caste mingle in careless unity at the National Congresses; inter-caste marriages are announced every day. Anyone who cares to look may see Hindus of every caste eating together, working together, playing together, or sitting together at the theatre, with no consciousness of caste.*[39]

But Untouchability is real. Even today, in some parts of India, the Outcastes are excluded from temples, public wells, and certain roads. A hundred organizations have extended helping hands to them; but until industry multiplies wealth and gives them a share of it, they will be too poor to be clean, and too dirty to be free. Their liberation is coming to them from above, from the campaigns waged for them by the Brahmo-Somaj, the Arya-Somaj, the Christian churches, and Gandhi,[40] and from the schools established by the Government under Hindu initiative.[41] In 1917 the number of Outcaste scholars in the schools was 195,000; in 1926 it was 667,000.[42] Under Gandhi's influence Brahmins and Pariahs have fraternized in many places.[43] India changes slowly. But every day the tempo quickens; and any day India may decide to become a modern state.

It might have been supposed that these reforms would receive every aid and encouragement

* I found myself, one afternoon at Madras, sitting with several Hindus, when it occurred to me to ask to what caste they severally belonged. They answered, smiling indulgently, that they no longer paid any attention to such distinctions. It is possible, however, that this was an exceptional, not a typical, experience.

from the British Government in India. Strange to say, it opposed them almost without exception. "In legislation upon matters of social reform the Indian Government has always thrown its weight upon the side of the *status quo*. The social reform movement has had to work without any countenance from officials."[44] The bill to raise the age of consent was resisted by the Government for many years; the bill for universal primary education was defeated by the Government in 1911 and in 1916.[45] "The laws as they are administered today uphold these superstitions" (the disabilities of the Outcastes), "and punish the Untouchables who dare to disregard them. Whenever a member of the Depressed Classes attempts to enforce his civic rights, the law steps in under the guise of preserving the peace."[46] "The British Government has always been friendly to caste; . . . first, because this policy tended to win the favor of the Brahmins, . . . and second, because caste divisions (or other divisions) tend to make the British task of holding the people in subjection more easy, on the principle of 'divide and govern.' "[47] The Government excuses itself by proclaiming its desire not to interfere with Hindu religion; but the Hindus themselves, in many of the Native States, have inaugurated moral and social reforms many years before these were accepted by the Government of British India.[48] Let an English clergyman and professor, the Rev. C. F. Andrews, sum up the matter:

> It has been my daily experience for nearly a quarter of a century to watch the course of events in India with an eager longing for advance in humanitarian directions. Every day my own convictions—slowly and painfully formed—have grown stronger, that the rule of the foreigner is now definitely standing in the way of helping social reform. In the Legislative Councils the official note is continually given for reaction. . . . If the British rule were to cease to-morrow, the advancement of the Depressed Classes would at once be brought into the foreground of the national program. . . . In social reform work in India it is probably true that progress would be doubly rapid if Indian statesmen had the helm instead of British.[49]

3. Greek Gifts

Even that economic development which has been held up to India as the dire prerequisite of her freedom has been retarded by English control. It is true that the Government, on a smaller scale than the old rulers of India,[50] constructed irrigation works, and then charged so much for the water these supplied that the peasants were in many cases as badly off as before.[51] It is true that new areas have been opened for cultivation to new over-taxed paupers, and that far greater areas have been lost to cultivation by cutting down huge tracts of wooded land, failing to reforestate, and thereby converting fertile regions into arid wastes.[52] It is true that India has imported silver and gold, and that this has largely gone into the Native States to adorn idle princes maintained by British power. A Hindu historian has shown that this influx of gold falls far short of accounting for the gaping discrepancy between exports and imports;[53] and an English economist has calculated that after making full allowance for the import of precious metal, "the yearly drain from British India of commercial products for which there is no commercial return," amounts to "upward of $150,000,000 a year."[54]

It is true that industries have been introduced to take advantage of sweated labor, and that the native industries of India were killed by English control of the Hindu tariff. The industrialization for lack of which India is censured was stifled in its growth by act of Parliament. The railroads, which have so helped British commerce and the British army, have been a drain on the treasury; their losses have been made up, year after year, from the taxes of the people. The worst famines in Indian history have come since the building of the railways, which were supposed to relieve famine.[55] "The year 1897-98," says Professor Dutt, "was a year of widespread famine in India, and millions of people died of starvation. Nevertheless, the land revenue was collected to the amount of $85,000,000, and cultivators paid it largely by selling their food-grain, which was exported to the amount of $50,000,000 in that calamitous year."[56] Today, after all these economic contributions of England to India, "personal observation," says an Englishman, "would lead me to the opinion that India's poverty is becoming more acute."[57] And an experienced American traveler reports: "The Hindu people impress the visitors as woe-begone and melancholy. One never hears a laugh, and rarely sees even a deprecating smile."[58] Is it not time that England should be called to account for what she has done, and not done, in India, these one hundred and fifty years?

It is said that England has given India unity. On the contrary she has delayed unity by supporting the caste system, and setting up puppet princes in seven hundred "independent" Native States, upon whose autocratic rulers Britain can rely to oppose the unification of India under a democracy. The Simon Report recommends further disunity by proposing the almost complete independence of each province; its secret purpose again is to "divide and rule." India has two hundred languages, or rather dialects; so has Russia; so has non-Russian Europe, which is no larger than India; Canada, with one-thirtieth of India's population, has 178.[59] Already 200,000,000 of India's 320,000,000 speak Hindustani.[60] For thousands of years India has had a unity far deeper than that of language or government; she has had the moral and cultural unity of Europe in the Middle Ages—that Europe which lost its unity when modern nationalism began.[61] Only self-government can give India political solidarity.

It is said that England has given India law and order and peace. That is, she has annexed state after state of India by superior killing, called victories; she has used India's manhood in 111 wars; and she has shot down or imprisoned those Hindus who dared to suggest that this was not law, or order, or peace. She has allowed the Hindus the privilege of fighting for every cause but their own; she has made a wilderness and called it peace. There is not an American in America who would not prefer chaos to such peace.

There are riots between Moslems and Hindus in India. But only in the British provinces; strange to say, they are rare in the Native States.[62] "In the case of many of these disturbances," says the always kindly and careful Gandhi, "we hear of Government agents being at the back of them. The allegation, if true, would be painful to me, not surprising."[63] Ramsay MacDonald writes of the "suspicion that sinister influences have been and are at work on the part of the Government; that Mohammedan leaders have been and are inspired by certain British officials, and that these officials, of malice aforethought, sow discord between the Mohammedan and Hindu communities."[64] Lord Olivier, Secretary of State for India under the first MacDonald Government, said: "No one with a close acquaintance with Indian affairs will be prepared to deny that on the whole there is a predominant bias in British officialdom in favor of the Moslem community, partly on the ground of closer sympathy, but more largely as a make-weight against Hindu nationalism."[65] It is a secret known to all that the removal of the capital from Calcutta to Delhi was aimed to secure the support of the Moslems against the Hindus. The system of communal or sectarian elections, by which religious groups in India vote as a unit, for members of their own sect exclusively, has intensified these divisions. The Simon Report proposes to continue this system, and lauds England for conferring unity on India.

All in all, the transference of British law to India has probably done more good than harm. The English judiciary, at home and abroad, are usually men of high character; and the admission of all castes to equality before the law has immensely stimulated India. In practice these virtues are slightly dimmed by the complexity and costliness of the new code; the simple Panchayats, or village communities, which once decided disputes and maintained order, have been replaced by a legal system intelligible only to lawyers, slow in its operation (important civil cases usually last five years), and prohibitive in cost to any low-caste Hindu.[66] The system has benefited the lawyers more than the people.[67] And while justice may be relied upon in cases involving only Europeans or only natives, in cases involving the two races justice is tempered with mercy—to the European. "Crimes committed by Europeans against Indians are always punished in the lightest manner possible, often so inadequately as to attract public attention and constitute a scandal."[68] An Englishman shoots his servant dead and receives a sentence of six months' imprisonment and $67.00 fine; a Hindu is sentenced to twenty years for attempting to rape an Englishwoman, while in the same province an Englishman who succeeds in raping a Hindu girl is acquitted with no punishment at all.[69] Says Sir Henry Cotton, long an English official in India: "Assaults on natives of India by Europeans have always been of frequent occurrence, with sometimes fatal consequences. The trial of these cases, in which Englishmen are tried by English juries, too often results in a failure of justice not falling short of judicial scandal."[70] Pandit Motilal Nehru, for forty years a lawyer in India, charges that not one Englishman has been convicted of murder in India in the last 150 years; the death of the Hindu is always diagnosed as due to accident.[71] Mahatma Gandhi, the fairest and most truthful man in public life today, says: "In 99 cases out of 100, justice is denied to Indians as against Europeans in the courts of India. This is not an exaggerated picture. It is the experience of almost every Indian who has had anything to do with such cases."[72] When the Marquis of Ripon, as Governor-General of India, proposed a bill to remove from Indian law "every judicial disqualification based merely on race distinctions," his palace was boycotted by his own countrymen.[73]

As to British "protection of India"—let us keep our hypocrisy within moderation; what the English mean is that they have kept other poachers out of the field. British protection means that British battleships are in the harbors, British machine-guns in the barracks, and British bombing-planes in the hangars, ready to kill the necessary thousands of Hindus if India should seriously rebel. Granted that if English protection were to end, some other exploiter would step in; what difference could that make to India?

Far more honest is the claim that England has taught India democracy, and initiated it into the marvels and perils of modern science.* A Hindu

*** At Tanjore, in the courts of the great temple, a handsome youth sat studying a Western text-book of anatomy; he was a symbol of the Great Change—of the modern movement from faith to power.**

must confess that before 1857 India had known only unmitigated autocracy in its central government, and that it enjoys more peace and security of life today than under even the most enlightened of native princes or Mogul kings. The teacher has taught so well that now she resents the progress of her pupil; and scores of free Englishmen arise to point out to India that liberty is dangerous, and that only Europeans are fit for democracy. England forgets that only a small minority of her people could read and write when she liberated herself from autocracy through Magna Charta.[74] As Gandhi reminds us, literacy and intelligence are not the same; the greatest of Indian rulers—Akbar—could not read.

A host of observers testify to the high average intelligence, the extraordinary peaceableness and orderliness, of the Hindu people. Lord Morley spoke of the native officials in India as "in every way as good as the best of the men in Whitehall."[75] Earl Winterton, Under-Secretary of State for India, did "not hesitate to say," in 1927, "that in culture and in education the leading men among the Hindus are not behind the public men of any country."[76] Dr. V. H. Rutherford, comparing his fellow-members of the House of Commons with the Hindu members of the national and provincial legislatures of India, found "a definite inferiority among the Englishmen compared with the Indians."[77] J. P. Spender, editor of the *Westminster Gazette*, said in 1927: "There is no eastern country which has so many talented men in so many walks of life as India."[78] Sir Michael Sadler, President of the Calcutta University Commission, said in 1919 that "as for brain-power, there is that in India which is comparable with the best in our country"; in spiritual qualities he ranked the Hindus above the British.[79] The Simon Report remarks: "We have seen several of the Provincial Councils in session, and have been impressed both with the dignity and the businesslike conduct of their proceedings."[80] And Romain Rolland tells us: "I have not found, in Europe or in America, poets, thinkers and popular leaders equal, or even comparable, to those of India today."[81] Travelers are amazed at the ability with which the elected representatives of the lowest castes are governing Madras. The courage, intelligence, and patient co-operation of the Hindu leaders in the Nationalist movement are sufficient proof that there is in India abundant talent to ensure a stable government. And perhaps disorderly self-government could be no worse than an orderly and dishonorable slavery, which undermines the pride and character of a people, and makes it ever more unfit for independence. Chaos is better than emasculation.

It is regrettable that India has become an economic necessity to British merchants and financiers. However, it was not India that brought about this situation; nor do we usually consider the inconvenience caused to the robber as an argument against the restoration of stolen goods. If a Hindu tariff controlled by India would injure British industry, let England recall the destruction worked upon Indian industry by a Hindu tariff dictated in England. Gandhi has long since promised, every responsible Hindu group has promised, that in establishing Home Rule "full guarantees" are "to be given for all vested rights justly acquired."[82] But the workingmen of England must not be deceived into supposing that they have profited from the subjection of India. They have never been allowed to share in the spoils; they have been as poorly paid while England sold their sweated products to India as were the workers of countries having no colonies and no empires.[83] Who knows but that an India free and growing would not soon double the imports now bought from England by an India impoverished and enslaved? Perhaps it is the prosperity of the East that is needed to restore the trade of the dying West?

As to the political implications of Hindu freedom, they cannot be too complex for adjustment between peoples agreed on mutual consideration. Rather it is the continued subjection of India that may bring problems incapable of solution. Not merely that imperialism becomes ever more costly as "backward" nations become more advanced, and exploitation exacts an almost ruinous expenditure on armies, navies, and propaganda—consider the money being spent at present to form and control American public opinion about India. But the compulsory retention of an unfriendly India within the British Empire requires a supreme navy, which taxes more and more the finances of Britain, and compels America to tax herself in naval rivalry.

Sooner or later the bondage of India will cause other wars as it caused the last. Every student knows that it was the threat of a Berlin-to-Baghdad Railway that decided England to enter the Great War. Historians know that it was the fear of a French march through Egypt to India that made England fight until the power of Napoleonic France was destroyed; and that the mixed marriage of England with Turkey in the Crimean War was due to British fear that a victorious Russia would stretch a paw through Persia and Afghanistan into India.[84] Let British workers realize that it was for this that a million of them were killed in the Great War—not for the rights and self-determination of small nations, but for the continued enslavement of great peoples. As Gandhi has put it: "The late War . . . was a war for dividing the spoils of the exploitation of the weaker races,—otherwise euphemistically called 'world commerce' "; and he remarks, elsewhere: "The greatest menace to the world today is the growing, exploiting, irresponsible imperialism which through the enslavement of India is threatening the independent existence and expansion of the weaker races of the world."[85] If that is so, nothing can be added to the conclusion of Lajpat Rai: "India holds in her hands the remedy for this universal misfortune, for she is the keystone of the arch of imperialism. Once India is free, the whole edifice will collapse. The best guarantee for the freedom of Asia and the peace of the world is a free, self-governing India."[86]

CONCLUSION

WITH MALICE TOWARD NONE

I have tried to express fairly the two points of view about India, but I know that my prejudice has again and again broken through my pretense at impartiality. It is hard to be without feeling, not to be moved with a great pity, in the presence of 320,000,000 people struggling for freedom, in the presence of a Tagore, a Gandhi, a Sir Jagadis Chandra Bose, a Sarojini Naidu, fretting in chains; there is something indecent and offensive in keeping such men and women in bondage. To be neutral in this matter is to confess that we have lost every hope and every ideal, and that our American experiment, and indeed all human life, have become meaningless. Our gratitude for our own national liberty, for the opportunity which our Revolution gave us to develop ourselves in freedom, obliges us to wish well to the Washingtons and Jeffersons, the Franklins and Freneaus and Tom Paines, of India. We may still believe that taxation without representation is tyranny.

Nevertheless it would be unwise to seek now complete independence for India, or complete democracy; universal suffrage should wait upon universal education, and complete independence has been made impossible by the international character of modern economic life. The British Empire is still a magnificent organization, an area of order and safety in a chaotic world whose lanes of commerce may at any time be infested again with bandits on land and pirates on the sea; it is good that these systems of order and internal peace should exist, if their component parts can be left honorably free. Once security required isolation; now it requires co-operation. We may even find something forgivable in the grandiose will of Cecil Rhodes, who announced, as his ideal and aim,

> the extension of British rule throughout the world, the occupation by British settlers of the entire continent of Africa, the Holy Land, the valley of the Euphrates, the whole of South America, the ultimate recovery of the United States of America as an integral part of the British Empire; the inauguration of a system of colonial representation in the Imperial Parliament, which may tend to weld together the disjointed members of the Empire; and, finally, the foundation of so great a power as to hereafter render war

impossible, and to promote the best interests of humanity.[1]

Our incorrigible prejudice moves us to prefer a free association of the English-speaking peoples as against the absorption of South or North America into the British Empire. We admire the Empire, but we hope for the day when it will be a Commonwealth of Free Nations. We believe that India's safest place in this acquisitive and murderous world is within that British Commonwealth; for a long time to come it will need British aid against invasion, against land-hungry native princes, and against religious fanaticism within. It should be willing to make a fair return for that aid, by agreeing to accept a diminishing foreign control for another decade, and by giving guarantees that Home Rule will do no injury to established foreign investments, or legitimate trade, or religious minorities, or existing governments in the Native States.[2] There is no doubt that a sudden grant of Home Rule, with a demand that India attend at once to her own problems of order and defense, might plunge her into such chaos as now disrupts China and helps to impoverish the world. The mob must not be let loose, for the mob can only destroy; one China at a time is enough. It must be remembered, however, that neither Canada nor Australia nor New Zealand was able to defend itself alone when, as long ago as 1846-56, they were given the status of free dominions. There is no reason why India, with one-third of her population composed of fighting races like the Sikhs, the Rajputs, the Pathans and the Mahrattas, should not have within ten years one of the bravest armies in the world. The Hindus fought well for France in Flanders, and for England in Palestine; they would fight better yet for the Hindus in India.

Therefore, though Home Rule must not come over night, neither must it be much longer delayed; for it may be as vital to England as to India. To India it will mean at last full opportunity for self-respect and growth; for self-protection in industry, tariff, taxation and trade; for self-reform in religion, morals, education and caste; and for the free development of a unique and irreplaceable civilization. To England it will mean a dominion saved; for an India longer forced under a hated yoke may abandon the methods of Gandhi for those of Lenin, and turn all Asia into a mad revolt against everything European or American. Already China is in flames;

Islam in Turkey, Persia and Afghanistan is rebellious, and Russia is at India's gates. The British Empire, if it continues to be based upon force, will consume England in taxes and wars; if it can transform itself into a commonwealth of free nations it will be stronger than ever before. The Revolution may be suppressed successfully today, but it will break out again tomorrow; its causes are wrongs far worse than those which led Ireland to bloody revolt, and lost America to England. These causes continuing, the Revolution will go on; and England will find it troublesome to put 320,000,000 people into jail. Let her remember that Campbell-Bannerman saved South Africa for the Empire by giving it liberty.

Would India be content with Home Rule? Despite all that has happened, all the high demands that are put forward as a prop to bargaining, there is every reason to believe that Gandhi could still be brought back, without difficulty, to the view he expressed some years ago. "A true relation between the British people and the Indian people," he said, "does not necessarily imply an India outside of the British Empire."[3]

It is a situation profoundly interesting, for it represents the most extensive effort ever made to test the practicability of Christianity. "Probably for the first time in history," says an American missionary, "a nation in the attainment of its national ends has repudiated force, and has substituted suffering, or what it calls 'soul-force.' Who can say that this is not more Christian than the ordinary attitude we have taken in the West?"[4] It is an astonishing thing, after all, that this "heathen" nation should be inflamed with devotion to a leader and a cause dedicated to *ahimsa*—non-violence—kindliness to every living thing. If India should succeed, the stock of Christianity (by which we mean here the ethical ideals of Christ) would rise throughout the world; courtesy and peace would be in good repute unparalleled. Every moral ideal would be reinvigorated, and perhaps the age of cynicism and despondency in which we live would come to an end. As Gandhi himself has said: "If the Indian movement is carried to success on a non-violent basis, it will give a new meaning to patriotism, and, if I may say so in all humility, to life itself."[5] Yes, life would be dearer to us, it would again have significance beyond ourselves, if India should win.

To Ramsay MacDonald the situation offers such

a chance for nobility as does not come twice to many men. What an opportunity to speak the healing word, even if it should destroy him! Will he remember his promise, and keep it at whatever cost to himself and his party? He must go down in defeat soon; for what better cause, then, than for dealing honorably with India? Perhaps, if his measures for Indian Home Rule should be framed, with his customary caution and good sense, to ease the problems which Hindu freedom might bring to British industry, the ancient English love of liberty and fair play would see him through, as it has lifted him up now despite his heroic opposition to the War. What a chance for England to be England again!

As for America, officially it can do nothing; it must leave Britain to face alone and unhindered these issues that involve the very life of her Empire. But as individuals we are free to be true to our national tradition of lending a sympathetic hearing to every people struggling for liberty. Writers who are not mere dilettantes, not mere money-makers, bear a moral obligation to leave no word unturned until the case of India has been presented to the world. Christian clergymen who are still in touch with Christ will speak out unequivocally, time and again, for India, until their united voices are heard beyond the sea. Let them ferret out the facts and pour them forth among their people, until not an American will be left to stand by in ignorant comfort while one-fifth of mankind is on Golgotha.

"What is your message to America?" Gandhi was asked recently. He answered, modestly: "I would like, on the part of the people of America, an accurate study of the Indian struggle, and the methods adopted for its prosecution."[6] And Lajpat Rai, Columbia University student, founder of the Arya-Somaj, inscribed to America in the following words the great book, *Unhappy India,* which he left unfinished when he was struck down as he marched unarmed in a peaceful parade:

DEDICATED

with love and gratitude to those numberless American men and women who stand for the freedom of the world; who know no distinctions of color, race, or creed; and who prefer a religion of love, humanity, and justice. To them the oppressed people of the earth look for sympathy in their

> *struggle for emancipation, and in them is centered the hope of world-peace.*

What more could be said? How could we read these words without offering to India some sign of understanding, and gratitude?

NOTES

CHAPTER I

[1] For detailed exposés of Miss Mayo's *Mother India* cf.: Dr. J. T. Sunderland's magnificent *India in Bondage*, New York, 1929—so good that its circulation is prohibited by the British Government in India; or Ernest Wood's chivalrous *An Englishman Defends Mother India*, Madras, 1929; or Savel Zimand's *Living India*, New York, 1928; or—full of information, but difficult to secure—Lajpat Rai's *Unhappy India*, Banna Publishing Co., Calcutta, 1928.

[2] Sunderland, pp. 480-1.

[3] *Indian Year-Book*, Bombay, 1929, p. 44; G. Elliot Smith, *Human History*, New York, 1929, p. 360.

[4] Kohn, H., *History of Nationalism in the East*, New York, 1929, p. 350.

[5] *Travel Diary of a Philosopher*, New York, 1925, vol. i, pp. 302, 273.

[6] *Ibid.*, p. 256.

[7] Sunderland, p. 367. Similar evidence will be found in Dutt, R. C., *Economic History of India under Early British Rule*, London, 1893, pp. 100, 105, 110, 415.

[8] Zimand, p. 32.

[9] Adams, Brooks, *Law of Civilization and Decay*, New York, 1921, p. 308; Zimand, p. 34; Smith, V., *Oxford History of India*, Oxford,

1923, p. 505; Macaulay, T. B., *Critical and Historical Essays,* vol. i, p. 504 (italics mine).

[10] Zimand, p. 31.

[11] Dutt, pp. 18-23.

[12] *Oxford History of India,* p. 502.

[13] Zimand, p. 34.

[14] Macaulay, p. 580.

[15] *Ibid.*, p. 530; Dutt, pp. 32-3.

[16] Dutt, p. 67; Macaulay, p. 529.

[17] Dutt, pp. 76, 375.

[18] Macaulay, pp. 603 f.

[19] *Ibid.,* pp. 609 f.

[20] Dutt, p. 7.

[21] Macaulay, pp. 568-70.

[22] P. 498.

[23] Macaulay, p. 528.

[24] Dutt, pp. xiii, 399, 417.

[25] *Oxford History of India,* p. 332.

[26] Dutt, p. 10.

[27] Moon, P. T., *Imperialism and World Politics,* New York, 1930, p. 294.

[28] Sunderland, p. 135.

[29] Lajpat Rai, p. 343.

[30] Zimand, p. 46.

[31] Kohn, p. 359.

[32] Moon, p. 294.

[33] Sunderland, p. 133.

[34] Lajpat Rai, p. 333.

[35] Dutt, p. 370.

[36] Lajpat Rai, p. 311.

[37] Dutt, p. 373.

[38] *Ibid.,* p. 411.

[39] *Encyclopedia Britannica,* 14th ed., vol. xii, p. 167 a.

[40] *Ibid.,* p. 167 b.

[41] P. 167 c; Lajpat Rai, p. 462.
[42] Sunderland, p. 424.
[43] *Encyc. Brit.*, vol. xii, p. 167 c.
[44] *Indian Year-Book,* p. 299.
[45] Dutt, pp. 369, 371, ix.
[46] Lajpat Rai, p. 354.
[47] Sunderland, p. 15.
[48] *Ibid.*
[49] Lajpat Rai. p. 356.
[50] *Ibid.*, p. 362. This has been partly remedied by the income-tax, which does not affect the poor directly.
[51] Sunderland, p. 369.
[52] Lajpat Rai, pp. 344-7; Dutt, p. xiii; Moon, p. 291.
[53] *Encyc. Brit.*, vol. xii, p. 178.
[54] Wood, p. 188.
[55] *Indian Year-Book,* p. 28.
[56] Lajpat Rai, p. 346.
[57] *Oxford History of India,* p. 780; Moon, p. 300.
[58] *Indian Year-Book* for 1828-9.
[59] Dutt, p. 423.
[60] *Ibid.*, p. 234.
[61] Lajpat Rai, p. 395.
[62] Sunderland, p. 311.
[63] *Ibid.*, pp. 308-9.
[64] *Ibid.*, p. 486.
[65] Lajpat Rai, p. 481.
[66] Sunderland, p. 305.
[67] *Ibid.*, p. 306.
[68] Dutt, p. 321.
[69] *Ibid.*, p. 426.
[70] *Ibid.*, p. 414.
[71] *Op. cit.*, p. 90.

[72] Sunderland, pp. 376 f.
[73] Zimand, p. 184.
[74] Sunderland, p. 482.
[75] *Ibid.*, p. 170.
[76] *Ibid.*, p. 467.
[77] Zimand, p. 217.
[78] Mayo, Katherine, *Mother India,* New York, 1928, p. 374.
[79] Lajpat Rai, p. 355.
[80] *Indian Year-Book,* p. 29.
[81] Zimand, pp. 180-1, 9-10, 178.
[82] Lajpat Rai, p. 321.
[83] Dutt, p. 256.
[84] *Ibid.*, pp. 45, 256-7, viii-ix.
[85] *Ibid.*, p. 263.
[86] Martin, Montgomery, *Eastern India,* in Dutt, p. 290.
[87] Zimand, p. 191.
[88] Kohn, p. 101.
[89] Lajpat Rai, p. 382.
[90] *Ibid.*, p. 462.
[91] Sunderland, p. 365.
[92] Digby, *Prosperous India,* p. 208, in Lajpat Rai, p. 333.
[93] Dutt, p. 47.
[94] *Indian Year-Book,* p. 791.
[95] Lajpat Rai, p. 341.
[96] Dutt, p. 50.
[97] Lajpat Rai, p. 514.
[98] Zimand, p. 193.
[99] Lajpat Rai, p. 514.
[100] Sunderland, p. 300.
[101] Dutt, p. 49.
[102] Adams, pp. 259-65; Sunderland, p. 386.
[103] Adams, pp. 313 f.

[104] Dutt, p. xiii.
[105] Sunderland, p. 20; Lajpat Rai, pp. 341, 348.
[106] Dutt, p. 409.
[107] *Ibid.*, p. 420.
[108] Lajpat Rai, p. 357; Sunderland, p. 316.
[109] Lajpat Rai, pp. 24-34.
[110] Moon, p. 308; Sunderland, p. 259.
[111] *Indian Year-Book*, p. 398.
[112] Lajpat Rai, p. 78.
[113] *Ibid.*, p. 55.
[114] Sunderland, p. 283.
[115] Lajpat Rai, p. 69.
[116] Moon, p. 308.
[117] Sunderland, p. 259.
[118] Lajpat Rai, p. 42.
[119] Sunderland, p. 206.
[120] *Ibid.*, p. 160.
[121] *Ibid.*
[122] Pp. 146, 156.
[123] P. 149.
[124] P. 150.
[125] Lorenz, *Round-the-World Traveler*, New York, 1929, p. 207.
[126] Sunderland, p. 155.
[127] *Ibid.*, pp. 149, 151.
[128] P. 149.
[129] Dutt, p. 423.
[130] Sir William Hunter, in Lajpat Rai, p. 284.
[131] Lajpat Rai, p. 288.
[132] *Ibid.*, p. 353.
[133] P. 366.
[134] *Indian Year-Book*, p. 16.
[135] Sunderland, p. 12; Dutt, p. vi.
[136] E.g., Dr. C. C. Batchelder.

[137] Dutt, pp. 51-2.

[138] *Ibid.*, p. 7.

[139] From an address to the Bar Association of New York, in Lajpat Rai, p. 481.

[140] Sunderland, p. 140; Zimand, p. 173—the average for 1916-25.

[141] Mayo, p. 97.

[142] Sunderland, p. 158; Zimand, p. 179.

[143] Sunderland, pp. 140-1.

[144] Lajpat Rai, p. 350.

CHAPTER II

[1] Fülop-Miller, René, *Lenin and Gandhi*, London, 1927, p. 171. Equally good is Josef Washington Hall, *Eminent Asians*, New York, 1929. Of biographies I have found the best to be Gray and Parekh, *Mahatma Gandhi*, Calcutta, 1928; Romain Rolland's *Mahatma Gandhi*, New York, 1924, is a little vague and airy. Two volumes by C. F. Andrews, one on the career of Gandhi, the other on his ideas, are announced as this book goes to press; they will be of great value, since Andrews has been for twenty years an intimate friend of Gandhi. An autobiography entitled *Mahatma Gandhi: His Own Story*, has just appeared in England, and has aroused much comment by its candor.

[2] Fülop-Miller, pp. 174-6.

[3] Gandhi, *Young India*, 1924-26; New York, 1927, p. 123.

[4] *Ibid.*, p. 133.

[5] Fülop-Miller, p. 168.

[6] Hall, p. 408.

[7] Fülop-Miller, pp. 202-3.

[8] *Ibid.*, p. 200.

[9] Chirol, Sir Valentine, *India,* London, 1926, p. 213.

[10] Gandhi, p. 309.

[11] Fülop-Miller, pp. 208-10.

[12] Gandhi, p. 21.

[13] Rolland, p. 7.

[14] Hall, p. 396.

[15] Gray and Parekh, p. 6.

[16] *Ibid.*, p. 7.

[17] Hall, p. 400; Rolland, p. 40.

[18] Hall, p 402; Rolland, p. 11.

[19] Rolland, p. 16.

[20] Hall, p. 403.

[21] Fülop-Miller, p. 267; Hall, p. 413.

[22] Moon, *Imperialism and World Politics,* p. 290.

[23] Fülop-Miller, p. 205.

[24] Parmelee, M., *Oriental and Occidental Culture,* New York, 1928, p. 302; Gray and Parekh, p. 27.

[25] Gray and Parekh, p. 35.

[26] Rolland, p. 92.

[27] Kohn, *History of Nationalism in the East,* p. 404.

[28] Gray and Parekh, p. 64; Rolland, p. 90; Hall, p. 439.

[29] Gandhi, p. 179.

[30] Cf. Hall, p. 492; Gandhi, p. 13.

[31] Gray and Parekh, p. 109.

[32] Gandhi, p. 36.

[33] *Ibid.*

[34] Gandhi, p. 69.

[35] Rolland, p. 66.

[36] In Fülop-Miller, p. 259.

[37] Gandhi, p. 887; Fülop-Miller, p. 291; Hall, p. 493.

[38] Close, Upton (pseudonym for Josef Washington Hall), *The Revolt of Asia*, New York, 1928, p. 47.

[39] Gandhi, p. 279.

[40] Hall, p. 480.

[41] Hall, p. 440; Fülop-Miller, p. 281.

[42] Mukerji, Dhan Gopal, *Visit India with Me*, New York, 1929, p. 138.

[43] Fülop-Miller, p. 299; Rolland, p. 220; Kohn, pp. 410-12.

[44] Rolland, p. 224.

[45] Fülop-Miller, p. 177.

[46] Zimand, *Living India*, p. 223.

[47] Fülop-Miller, p. 315.

[48] *Ibid.*, p. 186.

[49] Gray and Parekh, p. 99.

[50] Rolland, p. 69.

[51] Fülop-Miller, p. 169.

[52] Rolland, p. 140.

[53] Gandhi, p. 29.

[54] *Ibid.*, p. 78.

[55] *Ibid.*, p. 314.

[56] Hall, p. 496.

[57] Park, No Yong, *Making a New China*, Boston, 1929, p. 293.

[58] Gandhi, p. 721.

[59] Gray and Parekh, p. 26.

[60] *Ibid.*, p. 29.

[61] Rolland, p. 36.

[62] Hall, p. 500.

[63] Rolland, p. 36.

[64] Fülop-Miller, p. 244.

[65] Gandhi, pp. 75, 183.

[66] *Ibid.*, p. 55.
[67] *Ibid.*, p. 73.
[68] *Ibid.*, p. 58.
[69] Gray and Parekh, p. 120.
[70] Hall, p. 437.
[71] Gandhi, p. 59.
[72] *Ibid.*, p. 78.
[73] *Ibid.*, p. 131.
[74] Hall, p. 474.
[75] *Unity* for August 18, 1930.
[76] Hall, p. 502; Rolland, p. 46.
[77] Zimand, p. 95.
[78] Rolland, pp. 38, 48.
[79] *Ibid.*, pp. 137 f.
[80] Gandhi, p. 60.
[81] Rolland, p. 133.
[82] Hall, p. 495.
[83] Gandhi, p. 652; Rolland, p. 49.
[84] Gandhi, p. 652.
[85] Hall, p. 503; Rolland, p. 45.
[86] Gandhi, p. 56.
[87] *Ibid.*, pp. 70, 74.
[88] Hall, p. 503; Gandhi, pp. 30, 70.
[89] Gandhi, p. 79.
[90] Fülop-Miller, p. 237; Parmelee, p. 89; Kohn, pp. 401-2.
[91] Fülop-Miller, p. 235.
[92] Rolland, p. 51; Hall, p. 497.
[93] Kohn, p. 413; Rolland, pp. 8, 114, 121; Hall, pp. 388, 495. For Gandhi's treatment of sexual irregularity at his school, cf. Gandhi, 125.
[94] Fülop-Miller, p. 238; Gandhi, p. 720; Rolland, pp. 54-5; Gray and Parekh, p. 29.
[95] Hall, p. 506; Fülop-Miller, p. 227.
[96] Zimand, p. 220.

[97] Fülop-Miller, p. 233. An Associated Press Dispatch of March 4, 1930, told how a band of men transporting machinery into Tibet were set upon and massacred.

[98] Fülop-Miller, p. 233.

[99] Joad, C. E. M., in *The Listener*, October 2, 1929.

[100] Gandhi, p. 683.

[101] Fülop-Miller, p. 242.

[102] *Ibid.*, p. 316.

[103] *Ibid.*, p. 220.

[104] Zimand, p. 219.

[105] Hall, p. 467.

[106] Fülop-Miller, pp. 171-2.

[107] Kohn, pp. 103, 431; Mukerji, p. 208; Rolland, p. 112.

[108] Besant, Mrs. Annie, *India*, Madras, 1923, p. 2; Kohn, p. 9.

[109] Gandhi, p. 59.

[110] Rolland, p. 244.

[111] Gray and Parekh, p. 92.

[112] Fülop-Miller, p. 301.

[113] *Ibid.*, p. 293.

[114] Gandhi, p. 925.

[115] Fülop-Miller, p. 251.

[116] Gandhi, p. 940.

[117] *Ibid.*, p. 910.

[118] *Ibid.*, p. 28.

[119] Rolland, p. 235.

[120] Gray and Parekh, p. 85.

[121] Gandhi, p. 225.

[122] *Ibid.*, p. 277.

[123] *Ibid.*, p. 376.

[124] *Ibid.*, p. 270.

[125] Fülop-Miller, p. 228.

[126] Gandhi, p. 284.
[127] *Ibid.*, p. 226.
[128] *Ibid.*, p. 629.
[129] Fülop-Miller, p. 220.
[130] *Ibid.*, p. 243.
[131] Rolland, p. 170.
[132] Gandhi, p. 887.
[133] *Ibid.*, pp. 61, 539.
[134] Fülop-Miller, p. 280.
[135] Hall, p. 450; Gandhi, p. 241.
[136] Rolland, p. 68.
[137] Gandhi, pp. 869, 2.
[138] Fülop-Miller, pp. 207, 162.

CHAPTER III

[1] Kohn, p. 109.
[3] Hall, p. 427; Fülop-Miller, p. 272.
[2] *Ibid.*, p. 118.
[4] Sunderland, p. 406.
[5] Smith, V. A., *Oxford History of India*, p. 780; Lorenz, p. 420.
[6] Hall, p. 426.
[7] Lajpat Rai, p. 378; Wood, p. 188.
[8] Sunderland, p. 435.
[9] *Oxford History of India*, p. 593.
[10] Sunderland, p. 289.
[11] Hall, p. 479.
[12] New York *Times*, September 10-11, 1930.
[13] Sunderland, p. 488.
[14] *Ibid.*, p. 489.
[15] *Ibid.*
[16] *Simon Report*, London, 1930, vol. i, pp. 149-50.

[17] *Encyclopedia Britannica,* 14th ed., vol. xii, p. 167 a.

[18] Sunderland, p. 427.

[19] E.g., *Simon Report*, vol. i, p. 148.

[20] Lajpat Rai, p. 407.

[21] *Ibid.*, p. 404; Sunderland, p. 231.

[22] Sunderland, p. 423.

[23] *Ibid.*, p. 450.

[24] *Ibid.*, p. 451.

[25] Gray and Parekh, p. 49.

[26] *Ibid.*, pp. 49-50.

[27] Sunderland, p. 438.

[28] Chirol, p. 208; Sunderland, p. 438.

[29] Chirol, *l.c.*

[30] Wood, p. 189; Chirol, p. 209.

[31] Gray and Parekh, p. 114; Chirol, p. 209; Sunderland, p. 422.

[32] Sunderland, p. 423.

[33] *Ibid.*, p. 444; Chirol, *l.c.*; Gray and Parekh, p. 116.

[34] Sunderland, p. 448; Thompson, E. J., *Rabindranath Tagore*, Calcutta, 1921, p. 55.

[35] *Simon Report*, vol. i, p. 249.

[36] Gandhi, pp. 183, 75; Zimand, p. 138; Wood, p. 375; *Indian Year-Book*, p. 30.

[37] *Simon Report*, vol. i, p. 27.

[38] *Ibid.*, p. 249; Lorenz, p. 326.

[39] Hall, p. 450.

[40] Rolland, p. 197.

[41] Lorenz, p. 324.

[42] Kohn, p. 420.

[43] Zimand, p. 255.

[44] Naidu, Sarojini, *The Sceptred Flute: Songs of India,* New York, 1928, p. xi.

[45] *Simon Report*, vol. ii, p. 91.

[46] *Ibid.*, p. 60.
[47] *Ibid.*, p. 36.
[48] *Ibid.*, p. 290.
[49] *Ibid.*, p. 18.
[50] *Ibid.*, pp. 21-3.
[51] *Ibid.*, pp. 175, 174.
[52] *Unity*, Aug. 18, 1930, p. 347.
[53] New York Evening *Telegram*, May 23, 1930; *Unity*, Aug. 18, 1930, p. 348.
[54] Chicago Daily *News*, June 20 and 22, 1930; *Unity*, Aug. 18, 1930, p. 349.
[55] *Unity*, Aug. 18, 1930, p. 348.
[56] *Ibid.*, p. 353.
[57] *Ibid.*, pp. 350-1.

CHAPTER IV

[1] The best statement of the case for England in India is the recent *Simon Report*, particularly Volume II. More interesting is Sir Valentine Chirol's *India*, London, 1926. Entertaining but unreliable is Katherine Mayo's *Mother India*—a brilliant piece of propaganda not to be taken without an antidote. The English histories of India, except those by Elphinstone and Vincent Smith, are patriotic apologies.
[2] In Lajpat Rai, p. 456.
[3] Cf. *Mother India, passim*; *Simon Report*, vol. i, pp. 38, 52; Lajpat Rai, p. 186; Lorenz, pp. 327, 405, 335; Parmelee, pp. 139 n, 117; *Report of the Indian Central Committee*, Calcutta, 1929, p. 383.
[4] Chirol, pp. 169, 176; Smith, V. A., *Akbar, the Great Mogul*, Oxford, 1919, p. 401.
[5] *Simon Report*, vol. i, p. 19.

[6] C. C. Batchelder, *Saturday Review of Literature*, May 24, 1930.

[7] *Simon Report*, vol. i, p. 21.

[8] Dubois, J. A., *Hindu Manners, Customs and Ceremonies*, Oxford, 1928, p. 305.

[9] Besant, p. 25; Hall, p. 422.

[10] Chirol, p. 176.

[11] Zimand, p. 174; Moon, p. 291; Sir George Paish in Zimand, p. 191.

[12] Dickinson, G. L., *An Essay on the Civilizations of India, China and Japan*, New York, 1926, pp. 18, 25.

[13] In Fülop-Miller, p. 243.

[14] Kohn, p. 358.

[15] Dutt, C. R., *Economic History of India: the Victorian Age*, London, 1903, p. 198.

[16] Cf. AE's (George W. Russell's) suggestive preface to Zimand.

[17] Kohn, p. 122.

[18] Prof. Rhys Davids considers the climate of the northern and more populous half of India to be quite healthy; cf. *Buddhist India*, New York, 1903, pp. 43-4.

[19] Until 1885 the age of consent in England was thirteen; at present it is fourteen. Lajpat Rai, p. 257. In twelve of the United States the legal age of marriage for women is twelve years. Zimand, p. 108.

[20] Mukerji, M. J., *A Son of Mother India Answers*, New York, 1927, p. 59; Sunderland, p. 499.

[21] Mukerji, p. 27; Sunderland, p. 254.

[22] Zimand, p. 101.

[23] Hall, p. 505.

[24] Wood, p. 46.

[25] Lajpat Rai, p. lviii.

[26] Mukerji, p. 31.

[27] Lajpat Rai, p. lviii; Sunderland, p. 247.

[28] For 1921; vol. i, p. 151, in Mukerji, p. 19.

[29] Zimand, p. 117.

[30] Wood, p. 33.

[31] Mukerji, p. 51. Dr. M. I. Balfour of India gives 18.7 as the average age of first maternity in the Bombay hospitals, and 19.4 in Madras hospitals. Cf. Lajpat Rai, p. 188; Sunderland, p. 247.

[32] Cf. Rabindranath Tagore in Keyserling, H., *The Book of Marriage*, New York, 1926, p. 112.

[33] Lajpat Rai, p. 192; Wood, p. 111.

[34] Kohn, p. 425.

[35] Wood, p. 117.

[36] Prof. Sudhindra Bose, in the *Nation* (New York), June 19, 1929.

[37] New York *Times*, June 16, 1930.

[38] Mukerji, D. G., *Visit India with Me*, p. 209.

[39] Sunderland, p. 204; "Upton Close," pp. 235, 176; Wood, p. 266; Mukerji, *A Son of Mother India Answers*, p. 38.

[40] Cf. *Report of the Indian Central Committee*, p. 375.

[41] *Simon Report*, vol. i, p. 395.

[42] Zimand, p. 103.

[43] Kohn, p. 427.

[44] Mr. K. Natarajan, in Sunderland, p. 254.

[45] Lajpat Rai, pp. lviii, 191, 69.

[46] *Report of the Indian Central Committee*, p. 375.

[47] Sunderland, p. 204.

[48] Lajpat Rai, p. 204; Indian Year Book for 1929, pp. 576-7; Wood, p. 175.

[49] In Sunderland, p. 257.
[50] Besant, p. 50.
[51] Dutt, *op. cit.*, pp. 173-4.
[52] Besant, p. 52.
[53] Dutt, p. 529.
[54] H. M. Hyndman in Wood, p. 412.
[55] Wood, p. 396.
[56] Dutt, p. 534.
[57] Wood, p. 235.
[58] Lorenz, p. 315.
[59] Sunderland, p. 216.
[60] Mukerji, *Visit India with Me*, p. 201.
[61] Kohn, p. 349.
[62] Wood, p. 361.
[63] Gandhi, p. 73.
[64] In Sunderland, p. 233.
[65] Lajpat Rai, p. 409.
[66] Zimand, p. 232; Lorenz, p. 322.
[67] Sunderland, p. 117.
[68] *Ibid.*, p. 121.
[69] *Ibid.*
[70] *Ibid.*, p. 126.
[71] P. 125.
[72] P. 127.
[73] Zimand, p. 51.
[74] Sunderland, p. 211.
[75] P. 334.
[76] P. 332.
[77] P. 339.
[78] P. 327.
[79] Mukerji, *A Son of Mother India Answers*, p. 44.
[80] *Simon Report*, vol. ii, p. 54.
[81] Preface to his *Ramakrishna*
[82] Gandhi, p. 436.

[83] J. K. Turner in Sunderland, p. 394.
[84] Kohn, p. 98.
[85] Gandhi, pp. 863, 62.
[86] Lajpat Rai, p. 425.

CONCLUSION

[1] Kohn, p. 94.
[2] Gandhi recognizes this last necessity; cf. *Young India*, p. 436.
[3] Zimand, p. 228.
[4] Dr. Stanley Jones in Gray and Parekh, p. 92.
[5] Zimand, p. 18.
[6] *Ibid.*, p. 228. May I add, in this last word, that I should like to see applied to Haiti and the Philippines the same principles of Home Rule which have been here defended in the case of India?